D1377903

SPK 230

Business and Professional
Speech Communication
Course Packet

Fourth Custom Edition for West Chester University

ISBN 10: 1-269-97253-7
ISBN 13: 978-1-269-97253-6

SPK 230 Table of Contents

* NOTE: <u>Write in this course packet... all the materials are yours to keep!</u>
This packet is meant to assist you in preparing presentations and course work for your SPK 230 class – along with any other presentation that you will give in a business or professional setting. Therefore, you will find here a variety of current resources to use, which the WCU Communication Studies Department will update each year. Please write on any part of this packet and put your name on it.

* NOTE: **Pull pages out for class assignments!**
Because students will pull pages out of course packets, be sure that you NEVER BUY A USED COPY OF THE SPK 208 OR SPK 230 PACKETS.

Part A:
2014-2015
Course Policies

* All sections of SPK 230 have some common course policies and guidelines, which are provided in this part of the course packet. Your instructor may establish additional policies and guidelines beyond the ones listed here. You should consult your instructor for your particular section of SPK 230 to identify the specific grading criteria and guidelines for your class section.

* All students of SPK 230 are expected to have a Desire2Learn (D2L) account, a West Chester University e-mail account that they check regularly, and access to both a computer and a printer (WCU provides access to all of this technology for registered students). The following material is common to all sections of SPK 230 unless otherwise identified.

Students new to D2L should familiarize themselves with the system by:

1. Using the WCU general information guide
   <http://www.wcupa.edu/infoservices/d2l/students/default.asp>

2. Going through the step-by-step brochure
   <http://www.wcupa.edu/infoservices/d2l/students/Desire2Learn%20Brochur
   e%20updated.pdf>.

* All technology issues must be managed by students in a timely fashion; SPK 230 instructors will not be able to assist with D2L access or posting issues and **waiting until the last minute to post or print materials cannot change due dates or deadlines** (these materials will not be accepted so please do not wait until the last minute when technology issues always will arise!).

Expectations for Student Conduct

Academic Misconduct: Academic misconduct will not be tolerated. Proof of academic misconduct results in automatic failure and removal from the course. Academic misconduct includes any act that violates the rights of another student in academic work, that involves misrepresentation of your own work, or that disrupts the instruction of the course. Academic misconduct includes (but is not limited to): cheating on assignments or examinations; plagiarizing, which means misrepresenting as your own work any part of work done by another; selling, purchasing, or exchanging of term papers or speeches; falsifying of information; depriving another student of necessary course materials; interfering with another student's work; being a disruption in class; or not participating (or not focusing on tasks) during small group exercises.

- **Types of Plagiarism:** Students should become familiar with the levels of academic integrity *before* crafting or submitting materials. Work turned in for this course is subject to significant evaluation for any types of plagiarism, as described by Barnbaum (see: http://www.valdosta.edu/~cbarnbau/personal/teaching_MISC/plagiarism.htm): **Type I: Copy & Paste, Type II: Word Switch, Type III: Style, Type IV: Metaphor, and Type V: Idea plagiarism**.

- **Class Commentary/ Behavior:** If your comments or behavior distract from the nature of the lecture – or your behavior needs regular instructor supervision and/ or monitoring, you will be subject to course removal (please see the WCU Undergraduate Catalog Policy on Disruptive Classroom Behavior in regard to the course removal process).

- **Use of Past Work:** Academic misconduct also includes using your own work from one class to fulfill the assignment for another class (without instructor permission and significantly adding to the body of information, changing the direction, etc.)

- **Class Etiquette.** We expect that you will be physically, emotionally, and cognitively present during both classes and speeches. Poor audience behavior (making speaker laugh, cell phone ringing, disruption, disrespect, etc.) will lower the audience member's grade and not that of the speaker. As common courtesy, please silence all cell phones and/or electronic devices during class or follow individual instructor policies on having cell phones or other electronic devices in class.

  Any individual entering or leaving a room during a speech can be distracting to a speaker. Follow instructor standards on entering the room during presentations – many professors will ask that you never enter the room while a fellow class member is making a presentation while others will simply ask that you enter as silently as possible. Never make significant noise (e.g., ripping out note pages, opening and closing zipper bags, etc.) during a presentation.

- **Email Etiquette.** The WCU code of conduct dictates that all email correspondence be conducted in a professional manner. Any abusive email to the instructor or to a classmate is considered academic misconduct and will not be tolerated. In general, use the following guidelines:

- <u>allow 24 hours for a response to an email</u> – email should never be used for last minute questions about assignments, notifications of missed class or needs *during* class time, or for questions that ask for an immediate response.
- <u>put your name in all email correspondence</u> – include course and section time for further clarity; email systems often do not clearly show message authors (even from one WCU account to another) so be sure to include your full name in your message and the time of your class.
- <u>be polite</u> – consider your tone and the content of all messages
- <u>act as you would in person</u> – never, ever say anything in an email that you would not say to the recipient's face or in front of others
- <u>use appropriate language</u> – never swear, use vulgarities, or any other inappropriate language in email or interpersonal communication

Grading Guidelines for Presentations

Overview:

All faculty who teach courses in public speaking and business speaking strive for consistency in grading speeches. It is important that you receive candid, honest, helpful critique from an instructor who evaluates your speech using an unchanging standard so that you can better understand your performance. The following rubric is used for grading speeches, interviews, group presentations, and overall course work in your SPK 230 class.

A	The student has demonstrated ALL the requirements in a SUPERIOR way (mastery of requirements demonstrated)
B	The student has demonstrated ALL the requirements in an ABOVE AVERAGE way
C	**The student has met ALL the requirements for the speech – this is the "AVERAGE" grade (and should be considered to be a positive evaluation)**
D	The student met some of the requirements for the speech
F	The student has not met most of the requirements for the speech (with the speech demonstrating a lack of preparation)

Part B:

2014-2015

Speech & Assignment Resources

* You should always consult your instructor before implementing any of the strategies suggested in these resources to make sure they are compatible with the instructor's individual philosophy of public speaking in a business setting.

Professional Business Writing

General Information

SPK 230 is a class to focus on, primarily, business communication in its verbal and nonverbal forms. Your resources and textbook primarily focus on these elements. You will, however, be asked to produce written work in support of your verbal and nonverbal communication assignments, thus, it is important to follow strict professional guidelines.

All business writings, like with class work, should be delivered in a professional manner. Professionalism is part of your assessment in this class as it would be in any business setting. The most basic level of professionalism includes:

- All work must be typed (unless specifically directed to do otherwise)
- No ripped or torn pages (including pages from spiral notebooks)
- Your name should appear on <u>all</u> pages – preferably in a header with page numbers
- Stapled (not "dog-eared" or paper clipped)

Failure to meet any of these crucial standards, unlike in a job where you would be let go or not allowed to advance when you do not meet criteria, will necessarily result in a deduction of points.

Professional Writing & Plagiarism

College is a wonderful place to learn to become an adept and professional writer. In order to do this, you must take your assignments seriously, which includes speech outlines, agendas, reviews, etc. You should follow the guidelines given verbally in lecture as well as those in this packet and assignment sheets. These will help you learn to write well, be evaluated well, and develop a skill that you will use for the rest of your life.

Not Using Others' Work: First, never use another's work except to support your own ideas. Use of another's work in a variety of forms is considered to be plagiarism and has serious consequences. Because many students have never been schooled on all of the types of plagiarism, use these resources to know how your work will be evaluated in this class and in your professional career.

- Types of Plagiarism: There is more to plagiarism than using another's word for word work and not citing that person. You will be subject to penalty regardless of your familiarity with the types so please become familiar asap to avoid repercussions. All of the following are types of academic dishonesty: **Type I: Copy & Paste, Type II: Word Switch, Type III: Style, Type IV: Metaphor,** and **Type V: Idea plagiarism**. (see: http://www.valdosta.edu/~cbarnbau/personal/teaching_MISC/plagiarism.htm or contact your professor for a copy of this article!!)

- <u>Professional Writing Elements</u>: Once you have crafted your own work, expect that your written document will be assessed for each of the following areas regardless of points noted for individual assignments:
  - All work must include a header (inserted using the heading function to appear on all pages – see your professor's syllabus for details on your class headers)
    - Most headers for SPK 230 should include: last name, first name, two word assignment title, instructor last name, page number (headers should be between 12 and 8pt font size) *do not put your social security number on your papers*
  - Do not use contractions (e.g., "don't," "can't" etc...) in formal writing such as papers, cover letters, outlines, and résumés – also apply them sparingly in verbal presentations to keep credibility high
  - Capitalize of proper names (e.g., PowerPoint, Austin, Bill Clinton, etc...)
  - Use standard font size and type (Times New Roman or Arial, 12pt) as well as margins
  - Grammar-check and spell-check your work using computer software to catch errors (e.g., dropped prepositions, passive voice, tense matching, etc...)
  - Proof-read for errors (feel free to use the computer for the above checks but know that they do NOT catch all errors and you must evaluate your work)
  - Demonstrate clear organization (overall and within paragraphs)
  - Select proper treatment of the formal and familiar (i.e., "Mr. Smith and I" rather than "John and I" as appropriate to the assignment)
  - Sexist language is never acceptable in any form. Use phrases that allow you to avoid <u>he</u> and <u>she</u>. In no circumstance should the plural <u>they</u> be used for a singular case of either <u>he</u> or <u>she</u>.
  - For the sake of clarity, embrace *effective* word choice
    - <u>A</u> is a word and <u>lot</u> is a word, but you should avoid using <u>alot</u>, which is not a word, and <u>a lot</u>, which may be two words, but is not descriptive. Try <u>a great deal</u> or some other word phrase.
    - <u>Effect</u> and <u>affect</u> are not the same word. <u>Effect</u> the noun is the result of some cause (anxiety causes several effects). <u>Effect</u> the verb indicates the causation of some outcome (The presence of anxiety effects a climate of silence). <u>Affect</u> the noun is a synonym for emotion (many communication majors display a great deal of affect). <u>Affect</u> the verb means about the same as influence (lack of confidence affects people differently).
    - The past tense of lead (as in *she leads her people*) is <u>led</u>. Don't be led astray by typing *lead*

- Use the word <u>which</u> only in a prepositional phrase or when set off with a comma, which is the correct way to use the word. Use <u>that</u> in all other cases.

- Contractions have no place in *formal* communication. Please do not use them in your papers but apply them sparingly in verbal presentations.

- Know the difference between <u>to</u>, <u>two</u>, <u>too</u>, (and <u>tutu</u>).

- Do not end sentences with prepositions. This is a mistake with which I care not to deal.

Elements such as these will help you with the clarity and accuracy of your message.

Verbal Presentation Resources

The West Chester University Department of Communication Studies aims to give you every resource possible both to allow SPK 230 to be a wonderful and useful class as well as to assist you in your future professional presentations. The resources that you will find here can help to guide you in that process. If a resource that you need is not part of this packet, just ask your instructor. We are here to help!

Feeling a Bit Nervous?

Most people who take a public speaking class fall into two categories: those who must take the course as part of a curriculum, and those who take the course to overcome some level of nervousness or apprehension about speaking in front of an audience. Some people are even in both of those categories. If this is you, you are in the right place. West Chester University's SPK 230 course is about providing you with a level of skill and comfort when delivering presentations or having verbal communication in business settings. In order to do this, it is helpful to discuss why you may be nervous and how to manage those nerves.

Importantly, you should know that almost all people who speak are nervous in some way. Some folks hate talking to big groups, others shy away from interpersonal settings, and others dislike meetings in small groups. Typically, you will have more anxiety in one area and less in another. Your apprehension may be very high to just a wee bit of tummy butterflies. Either way, more information about these nerves is the first step to diminishing their impact on you.

What is "Communication Apprehension" (CA)?

The most common definition is that CA is "the fear of <u>real</u> or <u>anticipated</u> communication."

What Causes Communication Apprehension (CA)?

There are four main causes of CA
1. Heredity – traits passed down to you
2. Modeling – adopted behaviors
3. Childhood reinforcement – loss of confidence
4. Skills deficit – not comfortable with own skills

How does CA affect Us?

There are both internal and external effects. Internal effects are those of which we as speakers are most aware and yet the audience may not notice. External effects cover more of our outward behaviors and actions as speaker.
- Internal effects (from extreme to minor) occur in two categories:
  - Psychological – CA is in our head!
    - Discomfort
    - Fright

- - - Inability to cope
      - Feeling inadequate
    - Physiological – CA affects our body as well!
      - Rapid heart rate
      - Nausea & Perspiration
      - Shakiness
      - Dry mouth
- External effects show up in three main ways:
  - Avoidance
    - Avoiding communication all together
  - Withdrawal
    - Not answering questions
    - Little communication
  - Disruption
    - This can show up as us calling attention to the faults of our own speaking as well as that of others

What Can We Do About Communication Apprehension (CA)?

There are a number of ways to treat CA:

1. Systematic Desensitization
   a. Work slowly to be more comfortable
   b. To do: Lots of small presentations

2. Cognitive Reasoning (Positive Visualization)
   a. Turning negative thoughts into positive ones
   b. To do: See yourself completing a successful speech

3. Skills Training
   a. Seek guidance and instruction
   b. Get help in preparing
   c. **Take SPK 230!!!!!!!!!** (or another speaking course)

4. Always remember... it is normal to be a bit nervous before giving a presentation!

Be sure to talk to your instructor about any type of anxiety. He or she will have tools and tricks to help calm your nerves. This class will provide you with numerous opportunities to speak, which is a key element in overcoming your nerves. Take advantage of these opportunities, including that to speak up during class discussions!!

Severe CA – Impacting Class Performance: Some students will have a severe case of CA and need to work with WCU to manage the requirements of this class. If you believe that you fall in that category, please contact the Office of Services for Students with Disabilities at 610-436-3217 to have your CA registered and so that we can make accommodations for your success in SPK 230.

Research Resources

You can use a variety of different sources for your presentations. These are dependent on the topic, the audience, the presentation purpose, and what you are trying to argue. Above all you want to be sure that your speech sources are credible and that you have been ethical in your use of them. While your textbook will also cover this material, you may want to just bring your course packet to the library as you do research and this information will help you conduct it.

Levels of Review Credibility

One of the best ways to determine the credibility of your sources is to see whether or not someone (who is also credible) has checked the information. These are the levels or kinds of review that will be given to a body of information:
1. No Review
2. Audience Review
3. Editor Review
4. Peer Review

** Details of each of these are given in your SPK 230 Textbook:

Sawyer, J. K. (2013). *Business talk: Sending, presenting, and receiving messages in a professional setting*. Plymouth, MI: Hayden-McNeil Press.

Evaluating Online (Website) Source Credibility

Different types of sources can be used depending on their purpose in the speech. Although the Internet can be a valuable source of information, it is often difficult to know the authenticity of an Internet source. Think about it—anyone can have website. Try to look for cues in the page to help you determine how it has been reviewed and the credibility of the information.

Websites with URLs ending in ".gov" and ".edu" sites *tend* to be more reliable. Also, *some* ".com" sites serve as the *official* website on certain topics. The important thing is to know who created and maintains the site, which can sometimes be ascertained by answering these questions:
- Who maintains the site (the publisher)?
- Who is the author of the information?
- Does the page link to credible pages AND vice versa?
- Can the information be corroborated with other credible sources?
- How current is the information?
- Does the source have a clear bias? Or take just one side of the issue?
- How in depth or breadth is the information (does it just skim the surface)?

Finding Source Information at WCU (EBSCOhost, etc.)

West Chester University provides you with a wealth of resources. These are your student dollars at work and you should make the most of all of them! Many of these resources are dedicated to helping you to find information and resources for your coursework (and these resources are not available to you once you graduate – unless you are a registered alum and using them on campus).

Students often believe that a quick internet search or Google search will result in an easy answer for their research questions. Easy? Perhaps. However, as we learned above, the information can be invalid, unreliable, deceptive, or even just not the best that you can find. You will see here some ways to ensure a more credible research foundation but don't be afraid to walk into the library and look for print resources as well. Books, government documents, and periodicals may only be available in hard copy at the library. Often these are quick to locate, and you can ask for assistance from a Resource Librarian (located on the entry floor of the Harvey Greene Library by the computers) who is schooled in these sources and there to help.

Eight Easy Steps to Searching WCU's subscription to EBSCOhost

EBSCOhost is not, as most students believe, a database. It is much more. EBSCOhost is a collection of MANY databases that specify in research areas – according to their own definition, EBSCOhost is "*a systematic collection of online databases.*" Numerous universities have subscriptions to this resource but each has a distinct set of databases to which they have subscribed. If you say, "I got it off EBSCOhost" then your audience will never know which database actually archived the information. Instead, you would reference the specific database, "I got it from the

The following directions will help you to access sources provided to you through West Chester University, and now available with EBSCOhost® Mobile™ on your smart phone!

Step 1: Start at the wcupa.edu homepage and click on the **Library** link

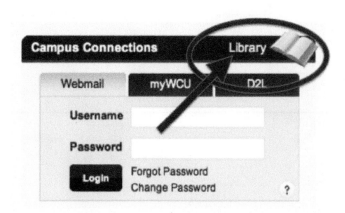

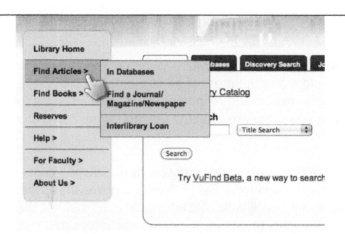

Step 2: Click on the **Find Articles** link in the left column and then select **In Databases**.

Step 3: An **Alphabetical Listing** list of databases will appear (as well as other listings). Click on the "**E**" to be able to select the EBSCOhost collection or click on the "**Select a Subject**" drop down menu to have the list filtered down to databases specific to your topic.

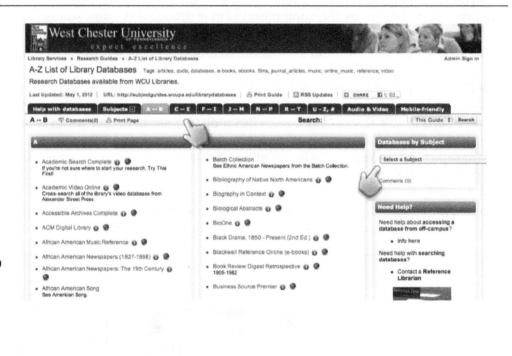

Step 4: Select EBSCOhost to view this system of collected databases.

*NOTE: If you are **off-campus**, you will now need to log in with your WCU ID and login. (This is the same login that you use for MyWCU or email.) THIS will bring up EBSCOhost in new window.*

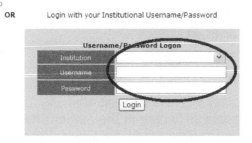

OR   Login with your Institutional Username/Password

Step 5: Select all databases that apply to your topic (as well as those that will cover or link to your topic).

WCU will have ONLY SELECTED ONE DATABASE FOR YOU (i.e., Academic Search Complete). It is a very broad database with valuable information on a variety of topics but you will need to check all others that apply to your topic! (e.g., Communication & Mass Media Complete, SocINDEX, PsycARTICLES, etc.)

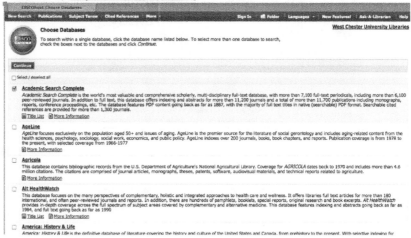

Hit "continue" to see the search term options appear (image below)

Step 6: Add **search terms** in particular select fields:	

Note: Use the drop down menus to **narrow or broaden** your search.	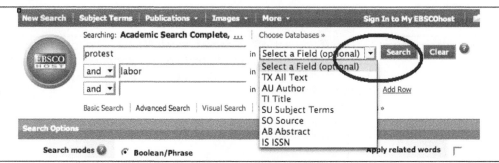

If your topic is narrow, consider using a very broad search; if it is expansive, consider using these elements to narrow your search effectively.	TX= the word appears anywhere in the article text AU= the word appears anywhere in the author's name TI= the word appears anywhere in the article title SU= the word appears anywhere in the article's listed keywords SO= the word appears anywhere in the name of the journal/ source AB= the word appears anywhere in the article's abstract (summary) ISSN= international standard serial number

Step 7: **View Results**	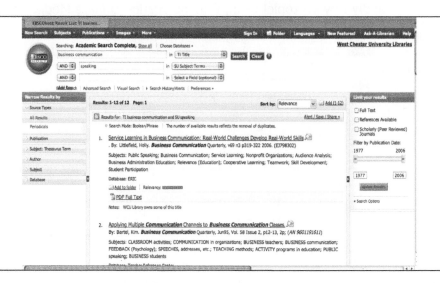

Step 8:
Narrow and Filter Results

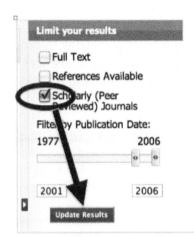

If you find that your results are too broad, not recent, or not delivering scholarly results – you can limit the results using the "limiting" box on the right of your screen. Check the desired boxes, drag the timeline to the spot desired, and click **Update Results**.

Additional (non-WCU) Research Sources

An online search may benefit you even if does not use a WCU resource. Consider looking at the most credible sources and using them in tandem with one another. Sources for additional information include:

- Google Scholar <http://scholar.google.com/>
- The Directory of Open Journals <http://www.doaj.org/>
- Project Muse <http://muse.jhu.edu/>
- JSTOR <http://www.jstor.org/>
- ipl2 <http://www.ipl.org/>
- The Library of Congress <http://www.loc.gov/index.html>
- Oxford Journals <http://www.oxfordjournals.org/>
- PMC (public medicine research) <http://www.ncbi.nlm.nih.gov/pmc/>

* (note that YouTube and Wikipedia are not on this list because the information there is not verified by an external source on a reliable and regular basis)

Now that you have your information, it is important to know how to cite it. For information on citing on your PowerPoint slides, see Part C of this packet, which contains the book: *PowerPoint Reality: Slides in Real Time for Real Audiences with Real Easy Steps* (Sawyer, 2010). For understanding how to document your information on the page and in your speech, just read on.

Why and How to Reference Cites

Sources in any communication medium must follow ethical guidelines to function effectively. We use them to create ethos (or ethical character credibility with our audiences) and if we use them with out verbally referencing the material then we are stealing or plagiarizing (a huge blow to your ethos).

In a class setting, your reference page enables your professor to trace the sources that you used while crafting your speech to evaluate there merit and your audience uses the verbal citations that you offer (hopefully these two elements correlate). Are your sources current? Are your sources non-biased? Do your sources come from the most credible review source?

Instructors will also use your reference page and your in-text outline references to make sure that you are learning how to avoid plagiarism – a serious concern that can have grim consequences. As mentioned a few times above, *you should not think of plagiarism as one means of "copying" but know how it exists in all of its forms*: **Type I: Copy & Paste, Type II: Word Switch, Type III: Style, Type IV: Metaphor,** and **Type V: Idea plagiarism** (see: http://www.valdosta.edu/~cbarnbau/personal/teaching_MISC/plagiarism.htm or contact your professor for a copy of this article).

According to the West Chester University Undergraduate Catalog (2009-2010), plagiarism is avoided when the source of information is "acknowledged through complete, accurate, and specific references and, if verbatim statements are included, through quotation marks as well."

Building Your Reference List (APA Style)

In order to document your research for your instructor, the last page of your outline should be devoted to your references. This page should have the title of "References" (no quotations) and be formatted using APA style, which is the standard for the Communication discipline. While MLA (Modern Language Association) style is most commonly used to cite sources within the liberal arts and humanities, APA (American Psychological Association) is most commonly used to cite sources within the social sciences such as psychology, education, economics, and communication studies.

The APA citation style is rather simple to follow once you learn the standard format (shown below). After that, it is just a matter of adding a few details. Some students will ask, "Why do we need to know all the details?" These details all offer cues to the reader about the type of material referenced and how to locate it. Once you know them, you, too, will find locating sources to be much easier.

In general, APA Style uses the following order:

Last name, Firs Initial. (Year). Title of the work. Source the work is in. Publisher of the source. Location that you found it.

See below for additional details and examples.

APA Style Guidelines Help

General Rules

What you will find below gives you resources for many of the types of information that you will use but certainly not all (that would take a whole book). However, there are additional resources and an entire book of details available to you. Look up all other guidelines and further details in the **APA 6th edition manual** and many questions may be answered through **the WCU library Citations Help page** – and try looking up your question online before asking your professor to give you the format (professors appreciate initiative and would far rather evaluate your effort and point you in the right direction than do the work for you).

As you put together your list, be sure to:

- Alphabetize each listing by the last name of the fist author (do not reorder authors)

- Italicize titles (not underline) titles

- Capitalize only the first word in a title or any proper name

- Only use first and middle name initials – not full names

- Do not have active (underlined) URLs on the reference page

- Look for authors of websites and information. A person should typically be cited but organizations will *sometimes* be the author (e.g., West Chester University)

- References on the outline (not reference page) need only be the author's last name and the year; for example: (Smith, 2010).

- Double space your reference page

Source Examples by Category (categories do not appear on the actual reference page)

article in journal
Smith, E. J., Ransom, M. V., & Tom, G. (2012). Psychological immunization: Theory, research, and current health behavior applications. *Health Education Quarterly, 17,* 169-178.

book
Hart, R. P. (1994). *Seducing America: How television charms the modern voter.* New York: Oxford University Press.

book on-line (two)
Sealey, G. (October 1, 2001). *A transforming moment: After September 11, young generations could see their world redefined* Retrieved March 27, 2002 from http://www.sos.state.ga. us/sac/18_24_articles.htm.   **(NOTE: break up URLs to not leave half empty lines)**

article from on-line source

Schambra, W. (October 21, 2004). Nasty politics? Puhleez! Get a historic grip. *Christian Science Monitor.* Retrieved June 5, 2003 from: http://www.csmonitor.com/2004/ 1021/p09s01-coop.html.   **(NOTE: break up URLs to not leave half empty lines)**
article from hard copy source but accessed on-line
Wiest, M. D. (2009). Toward a public mental health promotion and intervention system for youth. *Journal of School Health, 71*, 101-104. Retrieved August 25, 2001, from ProQuest database.   **(NOTE: do not give EBSCOhost URLs but list the actual database)**

survey data
Smith, J. (2012). [Survey responses to mental and physical disabilities in family history]. Unpublished raw data.

website
Canadian Lung Association. (2011). How to quit. *Canadian Lung Association* website. Retrieved May 26, 2008, from http ://www. lung.ca/protect-protegez/tobacco-tabagisme/quitting-cesser/how-comment _e.php.

interview – not included in a published paper (ask your instructor about inclusion for this class)

Willis, M. G. (Personal communication. August 15, 2012).

Source Examples as Seen on the Reference Page

References

Ahmed, C. (1998). *PowerPoint versus traditional overheads: Which is more effective for learning?* Paper presented at the South Dakota Association for Health, Physical Education and Recreation conference, Sioux Falls, SD. (ERIC Document Reproduction Service No. ED429037)

Anderson, S. T., Sr. (2009). *Multimedia in the classroom: Recollections after two years.* Paper presented at the Association of Small Computer Users in Education summer conference, Myrtle Beach, SC. Retrieved on February 17, 2012 from Communication & Mass Media Complete database.

Bartsch, R. A., & Cobern, K. M. (2003). Effectiveness of PowerPoint presentations in lectures. *Computers and Education, 41,* 77-86. Retrieved on January 27, 2013 from Education Research Complete database.

Biocca, F. (2002). The evolution of interactive media: Toward "being there" in nonlinear narrative worlds. In M. C. Green, J. J. Strange, & T. C. Brock (Eds.), *Narrative impact: Social and cognitive foundations* (pp. 97□130). Mahwah, NJ: Lawrence Erlbaum.

Bly, R. W. (2011, November). The case against PowerPoint. *Successful Meetings, 50,* 51-52. Retrieved February 3, 2003, from Communication and Mass Com database.

Blokzijl, W., & Naeff, R. (2004). The instructor as stagehand: Dutch student responses to PowerPoint. *Business Communication Quarterly, 67,* 70-77.

Hunton, J. E., & Bryant, S. M. (2000). The use of technology in the delivery of instruction: Implications for accounting educators and education researchers. *Issues in Accounting Education, 15,* 129-162. Retrieved on February 1, 2013 from http://papers.ssrn.com/ sol3/papers.cfm?abstract_id=232235.

(etc…….)

Example of Full Paper in APA 6th edition

It is often difficult to understand how these cites work in the context of a full argument such as a speech outline reference page or a paper. The following links gives you two different full papers along with notation of how particular elements of a work should be cited. While neither of these is a speech outline, they give numerous useful examples and there *is* a speech outline with references available within this course packet.

Please remember that just because an example is given here (such as a general dictionary) does not mean that use of that type of source would be acceptable in your speech or your class.

http://eulibraries.files.wordpress.com/2012/03/apa-sample-paper.pdf

http://www.apastyle.org/manual/related/sample-experiment-paper-1.pdf

2014 – 2015: SPK 230 Research Scavenger Hunt for Sources

Name: _____ Instructor: _____

Topic: _____ Desired Industry (optional): _____

This is a chance to put your research and citation skills to the test!

1. Select a topic
2. Go to the library and find information on your topic from each of the following source types and bring in FULL copies of each (do NOT copy into a Word doc) in a single binder:
   (note… the library charges 15 cents per copy – plan ahead and bring change!)
   a. **Book**
   b. **Hard copy peer reviewed journal article** (copy & staple full article)
   c. **Online peer reviewed journal article** (print & staple full article)
   d. **Editor reviewed magazine article** (print & staple full article)
   e. **Editor reviewed newspaper article** (print & staple full article)
   f. **Editor reviewed article from an organization** (print & staple full article)
   g. **"No review" or audience review information from a website** (no Wikipedia use or search engine results pages; print & staple full article)

3. Put the letter of each source on the article itself and put them IN ORDER in your packet.
4. Type up a reference page for the front of your packet that cites ALL of your sources (and then note which cite corresponds to which type of source)
   a. Be sure to use an APA header with your name and class listed

◻

References

Douglas, K. M., & Zachlin, D. (2020). It's time to decide: Persuasive strategies that

influence decision making. The Cialdini Society. Accessed on November 10, 2012

from www. cialdinisociety/research/_stratgies.html. (**F – from organization**).

Basil, M. (2011). A theoretical approach to evaluating educational television viewing.

Communication Research, 21, 177-207. (**B – hard copy of peer review**).

   b. On the bottom of your paper, type the library's hours for your semester and any other professor requested information! ☺

Creating Oral Source Citations

Sources should be clearly cited in your outline with the source names and years, such as "- 94% contagious (Smith, 2013)," on your reference page with full details (see above), and they should be cited within the speech itself. Using sources can make your ideas more believable, your argument more persuasive, and/or give you credibility as someone who is knowledgeable on the subject. The format used for orally citing sources is different from the format for citing sources in written form because verbal and written communication has specific needs.

When giving a speech, you must make sure that your audience understands enough about your source that the source credibility is clear. This does not mean a full citation should be said aloud but it is necessary that you "qualify" your sources/ advertise the source's credibility if there is any reason that your audience will not know the source (e.g., no reason to qualify "President Obama" but, who the heck is "Smith 2013").

Your audience should be able to answer:
- What are the author's credentials?
- From what specific publication or source is the information taken?
- What date was the information generated, published, or last updated?

For clarity, always state WHO before WHAT. That means that you say your source, qualify it, and then tell us what the source said. If you wait until after the information is stated, you leave your audience wondering how far back the source applies. Was it to the last sentence? The last two sentences? Farther back. Up front sources set up the audience for a clear relationship between information and source.

Example Formats for Verbal Cites

Introducing sources should be done purposefully. This means that you must organize your statements and use appropriate language based on the nature of the source material and the idea that it is supporting.

A.   "According to (citation/ qualification), yada, yada, yada is blah, blah, blah."
- **'According to....' is probably the most OVERUSED and least meaningful way to introduce a source into your speech.** The role that the information is intended to play in supporting your idea will not be clear. This is okay when that role is blatantly obvious AND you have not said 'According to....' a whole bunch in your speech. Otherwise, try to avoid this worn out phrase.

B.   Think about the strength of the evidence, the position the source takes or why/how you are using the particular piece of research.... and then let your phrasing reflect your intent. Consider the following:

- "Dr. Joseph Lightfeather, director of the Chronobiology Research Institute at Harvard University, agrees with me when, in the June 21, 2006 Newsweek, he said that 2 PM to 4PM are our least creative hours of the day!"

- "MIT Biochronologist Dr. Mary Wainwright, however, suggests in her newly published book, *Body Beats*, that creative hours vary depending on each person's unique body timer."

- "The editors of the New York Times just put out an article last Sunday where they argue that sleep is the least valued of our personal resources."

- "In a statement on the Tasty Cakes online home page updated June of this year, it would be a travesty to have this institution leave the Philadelphia area."

- "I had a chance on August 17th of this year to speak with Tracey Holden who is the inventor of fried ice cream, and I asked her about the mechanics of the process. She stated....."

- "Professor of Business Communication at Harvard University, Pamela Marshall, argued in a June 19th, 2013 lecture that it is nearly impossible to predict all of the outcomes of mis-communication in the workplace. She went on to say..."

- "I will have to disagree with Mr. Bill Garver, the owner of Strategic Consulting, Inc., who was quoted in Time Magazine last week as stating that political campaigns have limited resources. In the article, titled Where Does Obama Go From here?, by Ted Shecks, Garver argues that...."

As you can see, there we appeal to the notion of speaker ethos when we use our sources strategically to build our credibility. We can do this in any number of ways, the least effective of which is, of course, "according to....".

** It is worth emphasizing here, whether you use a direct quotation or paraphrase the idea, you still must give credit to the source where you found the idea. **If you don't, you are committing plagiarism, which is just as serious in a verbal form**. This is an ethical violation and constitutes academic dishonesty, which carries grave penalties. Consult your instructor regarding any issues.

Citing the Same Source... Again!

While you want to have as large a breadth of sources as possible, you may have occasion to repeat (different or new) information from a previously cited source. Rather than giving the credibility statement again, and since the audience now knows this, abbreviate the verbal citation as follows:
- "Dr. Mary Wainwright, the Biochronologist at MIT that I mentioned earlier, goes on in the same book to state...."
-
- The Biochronologist at MIT that I mentioned earlier, Dr. Mary Wainwright, also published an article in Forbes Magazine on June 10th, 2011 where she further substantiates that...."

Interviewing

There are numerous reasons to both conduct an interview and be interviewed. In general, interviews are two-way, task-related, relational communication organized as a planned conversation. Those who are conducting the interview are assessing/evaluating suitability relative to others. You are making a determination of your fit and comfort in the position. You will read a great deal about this process in your textbook, but here are a few additions to help you with the overall process in your SPK 230 class.

Interviewing for the Interviewer from Beginning to End

This class will provide you with communication skills for various types of interviews but as you prepare here are some resources to guide your process.

Before:
- Learn about the industry (read industry publications)
- Learn about the company
  - Conduct an informational interview with someone in the company
    - This is a good means of gaining visibility and prepares you for interviews with the company
    - To explore careers and clarify your career goal
    - To expand your professional network
    - To build confidence for your job interviews
    - To access the most up-to-date career information
    - To identify your professional strengths and weaknesses
- Do take a practice run to the location where you are having the interview or be sure you know exactly where it is and how long it takes to get there with traffic
- Practice your handshake
- Slowly acquire two or more outfits that are appropriate for a professional interview in your industry (a suit is not always appropriate and young and hip may miss the mark)

During:
- Be confident but not cocky
- Use vivid and specific language
- Never lie
- Offer names, dates, numbers, and measurements of your experience
- Do not interrupt
- Ask for clarifications
- Know your résumé (have updates copies with you)
- Have and be generous with business cards
- Know the job description *well*
- Practice how to answer all types of questions (see more on this below)

After:
- Send a hand-written "thank you" note to the people with whom you interviewed

- Send an email to all the people you met during your time on-site
- Follow-up if a deadline for them to contact you has lapsed

Dressing the Part: Business Casual and What That Means

It is impossible to give criteria for appropriate dress for all interviews. Professional dress is dependent both on industry as well as the specific company. Your best choice is to do your research. This includes asking and observing those in your desired industry.

Once you have done your research, do not just wear what they wear! Folks with jobs in your desired industry have already been through their interview and impressed. Also, what they wear on a regular basis represents a middle ground of the type of outfits that they will wear. Sometimes they will be dressier – sometimes they will dress more casually. You need to show that you have the ability to look as good as is necessary for the job. if your interview or presentation calls for "business casual" attire then consider the following details.

Too often, we are told that a professional setting calls for "business casual" attire. The gambit of responses to such a call for action appear to lead down paths from a dark suit sans the jacket – to cut off jeans (jorts – as one may call them) and even bikini tops. Most experts would agree that the correct attire is somewhere in the middle. Confusion about what to wear has had its backlash. According to Ellen Reddick (2007), "Too many people come into work as though going on a picnic or to a ballgame and employers become frustrated by having to correct behavior and don't want to take on the role of fashion police" (p. 9). The same goes for college professors who attempt to give guidance without having to judge the style of a professional or presentation outfit. These issues, however, lead us to the question: What does "business casual" mean?

The Ideal*
"It's the ultimate sartorial irony: Less restrictive dress codes were supposed to make life more comfortable for everyone. Instead, with the old rules gone, many people are in a state of dress-down confusion" (Field, 2000, para. 2). The notion of an ideal business casual look is quite general and does not take into account specific industries and situations as mentioned below... instead, it is a good general group of guidelines to follow when you do not know the above crucial factors.

For all:
- be clean and have well pressed (ironed) clothing
- avoid jeans or leggings
- no hats or hoods (no hoodies with or without hood up)
- no athletic shoes, hiking boots, or flip-flops
- limited jewelry/accessories or none (no ipod, earbuds, or visible technology)
- extremely limited or no perfume/cologne (avoid smoking and never cover smoke odor with perfume or cologne)
- avoid any distracting attire elements (including visible tattoos or facial piercings)

Women

24

- fitted but not too tight skirt (that itself or its slit is no more than two inches above the knee) or tailored slacks
- button down, collared shirt that reveals no cleavage and is not at all see-through
- muted colors (although a pop of color such as a bright shirt underneath a suit jacket can be appropriate)
- low heels that are not over 3 inches regardless of your height or flats (boots should be below the knee)
- nylons, tights, or hose are not necessary but are recommended in colder weather with skirts and in all conservative settings
- clean or muted color on fingernails
- small, tasteful earrings/jewelry/accessories or none
- natural toned and limited cosmetics

* for additional guidelines, see Layton (2011).

Men
- fitted but not too loose khakis or slacks with a belt
- long sleeve (typically), button down, collared shirt that is tucked in to pants
- tie or suit/sport jacket but not both, which would be formal attire
- no phone or wallet bulges (no phones on belt)
- any facial hair should be well-groomed
- long hair should (typically) be tied back
- socks should cover all skin when sitting and should not vary drastically in color from slacks or shoes
- conservative jewelry/ watch or none

* for additional guidelines, see Antonio (June 21, 2011).

Being Industry Specific

Every industry (e.g., educations, construction, journalism, law, media production, etc.) has its own version of appropriate attire and even appropriate attire for particular settings such as client meetings versus everyday work situations. The above guidelines are useful for when you are not able to find out the specifics of your industry but it does not mean that you negate the information that you are able to find.

Some industry acceptable differences may (or may not) include:
- women wearing a bright red lipstick and vivid colors in fashion industries
- men wearing clean, dark jeans in construction or blue collar industries
- clean t-shirts and athletic shoes in programming or media editing industries
- sweater-sets for women working in the office in law industries but collar-shirts with clients (and suits in the courtroom)
- women wearing black sequined blazer with jeans for an office celebratory event
- men in khakis and button down shirts in an academic industry but slacks and suit jackets at a conference or convention
- ugly sweater for a holiday party

Remember to find out any information about appropriateness that you can ahead of time and to always go slightly more formal than you would guess unless you have verifiable information to the contrary.

The SPK Evaluation Impact

The above details let you know exactly what is expected of you in business casual settings. Giving presentations in your SPK course will necessitate that you adhere to these standards but it is equally as important to know what happens (or should happen) when you are unable to or decide not to follow these guidelines.

- **should you be unable to adhere to these standards**: Some students may not have the means to adhere to all of the guidelines above. Speak with your instructor well before your presentation date; he or she may be able to help or discuss the consequences... after all, it is important to recognize that not being able to demonstrate the ideal will not result in ideal evaluations but an attempt to address the matter ahead of time will make a positive impact (remember that many of these guidelines are easy regardless of financial means such as clean and pressed attire with no distracting accessories – and a fair amount of items can be borrowed from friends or classmates).
- **should choose not to adhere to these standards**: As with any business issue or error, the magnitude of the error will determine the significance of the impact; you should expect not to be able to receive the highest marks in the attire area on your evaluation rubric and are subject to receiving the lowest rubric evaluation in this area. Regardless of circumstances, it is important that you know that less than appropriate attire will impact your marks on course evaluations just as it would in a professional setting.

The Professional Impact

Adherence to appropriate business attire has been well researched to demonstrate the following:

- **more formal attire is more respected**: young professionals prefer a more casual atmosphere but still correlate levels of professional attire with levels of authority (Cardon & Okoro (2009)
- **more formal attire is associated with more professionalism**: Some industries will expect more formal attire while others will be more casual but all have levels of professional dress that dictate how you re seen
- **more formal casual is associated with more friendliness**: more casually dressed professionals are seen as more friendly than formally attired professionals (Peluchette & Karl, 2007; Peluchette, Karl, & Rust, 2006)
- **more formal attire leads to better job satisfaction**: employees who prefer to wear more formal clothes themselves report a higher levels of time commitment, work intensity, feeling of fairness, conscientiousness, and job satisfaction as well as lower stress (Norton & Franz, 2004)
- **casual attire does not increase productivity**: there is no conclusive research to suggest that more casual comfortable attire increases productivity (Kiddie, 2009)
- **backlash from too casual attire is increasing**: companies who have seen too casually dressed employees are reacting by creating and enforcing specific policies (Field, 2000; Kiddie, 2009; Reddick, 2007)
- **formality is specific to industries**: what is considered casual in one industry will be considered too casual in another industry (Haefner, 2008)

You can find additional information from the references used for compiling this information (listed below) or go on to find more information that is specific to your industry and setting.

Cardon, P. W., & Okoro, E. A. (September 2009). Professional characteristics communicated by formal versus casual workplace attire. *Business Communication Quarterly,* 355-360.

Antonio. (June 21, 2011). 5 steps to upgrading your business casual clothing. *The Art of Manliness.* Accessed on January 2, 2012 from http://artofmanliness.com/2011/06/21/business-casual-clothing/.

Field, A. (October 2000 and June 2005). What Is business casual. *Business Week, 3705.* Accessed on December 14, 2011 from http://www.businessweek.com/2000/00_44/b3705141.htm.

Haefner, R. (2008, July 30). How to dress for success for work. *CNN.com.* Retrieved January 27, 2009, from http://www.cnn.com/2008/LIVING/worklife/07/30/cb.dress.for.success/index.html.

Kiddie, T. (September 2009). Recent trends in business casual attire and their effects on student job seekers. *Business Communication Quarterly, 72* (3), 350-354.

Layton, J. (2011). What does business casual mean for women? *TLC: The Learning Channel.* Accessed on January 2, 2012 from http://tlc.howstuffworks.com/style/business-casual-for-women.htm.

Peluchette, J. V., & Karl, K. (2007). The impact of workplace attire on employee self-perceptions. *Human Resource Development Quarterly, 18,* 345-360.

Peluchette, J. V., Karl, K., & Rust, K. (2006). Dressing to impress: Beliefs and attitudes regarding workplace attire. *Journal of Business and Psychology, 21,* 45-63.

Norton, S. D., & Franz, T. M. (September 2004). Methodological issues in research on business casual dress. *Journal of American Academy of Business, 5* (1/2), 130-137.

Reddick, E. (August 2007). Casual dress – the new elephant in the room. *The Enterprise*, 9, 15.

Adhering to these standards will help you to make a good impression, but only if your interviewer only sees you only is this appropriate fashion. Be sure to get dressed and put together away from the interview site. You never know who will be in the elevator or pull up next to you in the parking lot. Your best option is to be ready to go and "on" before the last turn in your drive to the location.

Answering Interview Questions

Once you are dressed and ready for the process, your primary task in interviewing will be your ability and skill for answering questions. There are many types of questions and numerous means of conducting interviews. You will find that some of those interviewing you will be prepared to ask questions and know your résumé well. Others will just wing it when you walk in the room. The key to success is to do your preparation and not worry about what others may or may not do.

Your preparation involves answering questions: *expected, dreaded, and illegal.* You should come up with as many questions in each area and answering them. Your textbook will talk you through the basics of how to answer questions and interact with your interviewer.

Asking Questions

For most of you, the thought of public speaking makes you nervous. This may be largely because you are unfamiliar with the process.

- What happened to the last person who held this job?
- What were the major strengths and weaknesses of the last person who held this job?
- What would you consider to be the most important aspects of this job?
- What are the skills and attributes you value for someone being hired for this position?
- Could you describe a typical day or week in this position? The typical client or customer?
- What are the most immediate challenges of the position that need to be addressed in the first three months?
- What are the performance expectations of this position over the first 12 months?
- How will I be evaluated at XYZ Company, and how often?

At the end of the interview, don't forget to ask the most important question:
- When can I expect to hear back from you? What are the next steps in the interview process? May I reach out to you in (amount of time) to follow up?

Employer "Google" Search
(adapted from J. K. Sawyer's "Google me?! Facebook You!" assignment)

The Case:
You are an employer. A job candidate has just applied for a job with your company. You have a résumé (provided by your instructor) but as of yet no other information. Before you interview this person... you want to know as much about that applicant as possible. Therefore, you will conduct an online search for that person and find out anything that you can.

(For example... you might have the name Carly Dobbs. Her résumé says that she is a West Chester University of PA senior in Communication Studies. You see that she had jobs in three local restaurants. When you go online you find that she participated in a 10K run sponsored by one of the restaurants, you find that she is a member of a sorority (not the one you were in! ☺), and you find that she is on the Dean's List at WCU).

You also go online and find that a Carly Dobbs lived in Delaware and headed up a volunteer drive. This might be her... can't be sure. You find a picture of a Carly Dobbs drinking and engaging in some outrageous behavior at a frat party in Maryland. This might be her... can't be sure. You next find a Carly Dobbs that lives in Paoli, Pennsylvania that is the grandmother of 9 boys. Pretty sure this isn't her.)

YOUR TASK:
These steps will give you general information about how to conduct your research but check with your instructor about the guidelines or requirements specific to your class/ section.

Producing Your Potential Employee's Online Presence Report – Steps & Documentation

Steps In-Brief:
1. Thoroughly Review the Résumé (see note)
2. Identify Search Terms
3. Identify Key Online Sites
4. Conduct and Document Your Search
5. Produce a "Hiring" Report

Be Professional in your reporting tone as well as respectful (this information will be evaluated and then give back to the "applicant").

Steps In-Detail:
1. Thoroughly Review the Résumé
   a. become familiar with the applicants interests and background
   b. note types of work experience
   c. look for special skills
   d. make a list of all possible links to the potential employee

2. Identify Search Terms
   a. create all possible variations and combinations of the employee name (e.g., Jennifer Smith, Smith Jennifer, Jenny Smith, J. Smith, etc.)

   b. if you have a résumé, take note of the following to combine with name searches:
     i. résumé keywords
     ii. regions or cities
     iii. company names

3. Identify Key Online Sites
   a. look for cited online experience or information
   b. select a general web search engine or engines (e.g., Google, Bing, Ask, etc.)
   c. select all applicable social media sources (e.g., Facebook, Twitter, YouTube, Friendster, LinkedIn, MyLife, Qzone, Habbo, etc.)

4. Conduct and Document Your Search
   a. search all keywords in all selected online sites
   b. document what was found in which place and the search engine/ keyword combinations found
   c. produce documentation
     i. print out the first page of all searches (i.e., to show search terms)
     ii. print out all findings
     iii. highlight the potential employee's name or information in the print outs

5. Produce a "Hiring Report"
   a. Write 3 single-spaced paragraphs that summarize:
     i. what was found (example: Facebook – comments and images, pg. 6)
     ii. what implications are made by the online presence
     iii. a rationalization for hiring – or not hiring – the potential employee including any changes that should be made in the online presence
   b. Attach all documentation and number pages for use as a reference from summary paragraphs

Consider....

- What surprised you?
- What *shocked* you?
- What would have NEVER posted?
- What do you wish to emulate as a means of navigating your own online presence?
- What communication strategies did you see used?
- How was online presence "managed" or not?
- What key rhetorical tactics could you identify?
- What advice would you offer the "applicant" and have you taken this advice yourself?
- How can persuasive strategies be incorporated into online presence?
- (more discussion to come in class...)

Résumés and Cover Letters

Your résumé and cover letter will serve as the foundation for much of your presentation work in this class. In addition, they both serve as foundational parts of Business Communication and must follow certain guidelines to work effectively.

Résumé Guidelines

Print
- Black ink (no blue, underlined emails) or clean, high quality laser printed color
- Check with your instructor about résumé paper requirements and issues

Consistent & Professional Font use
- In general: no more than two sizes in the body of résumé (typically 11pt font or 10 pt font... depending on the type of font style used)
- Typical legible font styles will be Arial, Times New Roman, Tahoma, or Calibri
- Names should be larger than other fonts
- Contact information can use smaller fonts but should still be legible

- Some emotional implications of particular fonts:
  - Serif (gloomy) / Sans Serif (easy going)
  - Times New Roman: stable, mature, formal, efficient, not easily read, serious
  - Garamond: classic, old fashioned, sophisticated, favorably judged
  - Arial: stable, formal, serious/ less serious than serif, direct, friendly
  - Comic Sans: fun, unreliable
  - Helvetica: stable, generic, bold
  - Courier: conformist, dull, unimaginative

(Brumberger, E. (2003). The Rhetoric of Typography: The Persona of Typeface and Text. T*echnical Communication, 50(2)*, 206-223.)

Contact information
- Name should be what you are called or full name
  - abbreviated names/ nicknames go in parentheses or quotations
- Must use Professional email as well as voicemail message
- Use a 9 digit zip code (research states that you will be seen as detail oriented)
- Only personal FAX numbers, emails, or phone numbers
- No blue, underlined emails/ hyperlinks

Education
- Must include all Graduation/ Degree Conferred dates (e.g., "degree expected" for current students)
- GPA should only be included if it is 3.5 or above
  - this can be overall or major GPA or both
- Know and write out your type of degree and full department name
  - *Examples*:
    - Bachelor of Science from the Communication Studies Department
    - Bachelor of Science; Department of Communication Studies
- List ALL schools attended (better to be up front rather than seemingly hiding something)
- Ok to include a brief list of *relevant* ONLY classes (if necessary)

Structure
- Never use a Résumé Template
- Employ either a Reverse Chronological Order or Functional Structure
- Use Categories that apply to <u>your specific</u> background
  - *Examples*: Relevant Event Planning Experience / Volunteer Positions / Leadership Roles / International Experience / Internships/ Research Projects/
  - <u>OK (if relevant)</u>: Honors/ Software/ Memberships (include role and dates)/ Language Proficiencies, Certifications/ etc.
  - <u>Not OK</u>: Personal Information / Personal Profile / Picture (on domestic résumés) / Skills Summary (unless executive résumé or significant experience)

(Schriver, K. A. (1997). *Dynamics in Document Design: Creating Texts for Readers*. New York: Wiley Computer Publishing.)

Clear Job Details
- Emphasize Job Titles (over company titles)
- List starting and ending month and year
- All jobs must include city and state (PA not Pa or Penn.) but not street addresses
- Descriptions should be specific to personal skills/ abilities (NOT a newspaper ad)
- Longest description(s) should be for the most relevant job (not necessarily the most recent)

Avoid
- "References Available Upon Request" or an Objective
- Full Company Addresses (these belong on an attached References page)
- Using the same 1st word or letter to begin more than one job descriptions (which causes readers to see similar rather than diverse experience and gloss over details)
  - Example (of what *not* to do):
    - Created excel spreadsheets
    - Crafted marketing tools for all upcoming events
    - Coordinated volunteers
- The phrase "responsible for" or "responsibilities"
- Any high school information (after freshman year) unless extraordinary

SPK 230 Résumé Evaluation Criteria

- All résumés must be delivered in a professional manner, which includes being turned in on time, in a clean manner, with clear effort to follow all guidelines
- Point Deductions/ Full Grade Deduction
  - Spelling or Grammar Error (even <u>one</u>)
  - Missing Contact Information
  - Résumé Length Extending Beyond One Page (for this class)
  - Lying (Equivalent to Plagiarism) will Result in a <u>Failing grade</u>
- Point Deductions/ Half Grade Deduction
  - Listing an Objective or "References Available Upon Request"
  - Listing High School information (that has not been pre-approved as "exemplary")
  - Poor print or paper quality
  - Typos (although a résumé cannot be given an A evaluation)

Résumé Example 1

Darlene Deliuth
423 South Avenue
South Wyoming, CA 18622
AM22222@wcupa.edu
(125) 555-7422

Education

West Chester University of Pennsylvania
Bachelor of Arts from the Communication Studies Department
Projected Graduation Date: May 2015

Sales and Marketing Related Courses Taken:

- Business & Organizational Writing
- Communication and Leadership
- Event Planning
- Public Relations

- Nonverbal Communication
- News Writing
- Persuasion

Professional Sales Experience

Consultative Sales Associate
Sears Holdings Corporations/ Fine Jewelry Department, Exton, PA   February 2011 – present

- Smile and greet all customers
- Display the jewelry in cases in such a way as to capture the attention of the customer
- Ask probing questions in order to better fulfill customers' needs
- Market cleaning products and care plans for all jewelry

Consultative Sales Associate
Sears Holdings Corporations/ Shoe Department, Wilkes-Barre, PA   June 2002 – December 2005

- Took care of customers' needs in a timely manner
- Kept all displays in such a way to grab the interest of the customer

Service Projects

Service Learning / Battle of the Bands Project Coordinator
Wyoming Area Secondary Center, Exeter, PA   February 2012

- Organized, promoted, and ran a battle of the bands
- Scouted a location and negotiated with the owner
- Worked diligently to acquire donations from local businesses
- Event donated sixteen hundred dollars to Wyoming Valley Alcohol and Drug, a counseling facility for people with abuse problems, for alcohol and drug abuse education
- Received honorable mention for this project

Friends and Family Night Event Coordinator
Sears & West Chester University, West Chester, PA   November 2011

- (Project as part of COM 499 Event Planning class)
- Designed layout and look of printed flyers
- Managed donation of baked goods donated with store associates
- Came up with creative activities for the event (e.g., as gift wrapping and pictures with Santa)
- Picked up needed items such as table settings and refreshments

Résumé Example 2

Michelle B. Willis

2478 Meadowswan Dr.	(202) 555-1999
Exton, PA 19375-2253	michellecrable27@gmail.com

Education

West Chester University of Pennsylvania
Bachelor of Arts, Department of Communication Studies
Degree Expected December 2015
GPA 3.7 magna cum laude
Dean's List: Spring 2011, Fall 2012, Spring 2012, Spring 20013; National Dean's List 2011-2013

Professional Training
Publishing Related Coursework (August 2010 – present)

◆ Computer Applications	◆ Persuasion	◆ Technology & Computers
◆ Cold Call Training	◆ Popular Culture Writing	◆ Topics in Literature
◆ Effective Writing	◆ Publishing	◆ Writing & Computers

Hands-On Publishing Experience
Aralia Press Trainee (August 2012 – December 2012)
   ◆ Learn traditional (by hand) publishing methods
   ◆ Publish original poetry by Pulitzer Prize winner, Richard Wilbur
   ◆ Set type, pull proofs, and print finished manuscripts
   ◆ Edit and format text in an appealing way

Hands-On Journalism Experience
Newswriting & Public Affairs Reporting (August 2010 – May 2012)
   ◆ Developed proficiency in the writing of news stories (including feature stories) for daily and weekly newspapers
   ◆ Learned the values of news, structure & style of news, and the preparation of copy with professional standards
   ◆ Assignments included coverage of speeches, local government meetings, & the courts
   ◆ Worked to meet deadlines

Professional Administrative Experience

Special Orders Assistant
Borders Books and Music/Borders, Inc., Camp Hill, PA   April 2013 – August 2013
   ◆ Personally worked with customers and publishers to obtain books otherwise unavailable or out of stock
   ◆ Organized special orders directly with publishers for customers (e.g., Harry Potter, assigned school readings)
   ◆ Managed all financial paperwork for special orders and corporate sales

Bookseller
Borders Books and Music/Borders, Inc., Camp Hill, PA   November 2012 – April 2013
   ◆ Used my knowledge and passion for books to help customers locate best selections for their needs
   ◆ Designed original displays on the sales floor to market products and new publications
   ◆ **Employee of the Month (April 2007)**

Computer Skills and Training:
(PC & Macintosh): Microsoft Office Applications/Adobe Photoshop, Dreamweaver/Webpage & Blog Design

Cover Letter Guidelines

A cover letter is used to make an introduction to an employer, introduce your résumé, and get an interview. They can be sent to find out about jobs, to reply to an advertisement, to begin communication with an employer, or to take action on a job referral.

Reminders

- Try to keep letters to one page only (for this class... no more than one page)
  - Know for what industries your cover letter should be more than one page
- Use three to four paragraphs (see the attached example for specific criteria for each paragraph)
- Type the letter, using 8 ½ x 11-inch, high-quality paper (matching résumé paper)
- Focus on what you can contribute to the employer (i.e., for that job – not just in general), including the experience, skills and knowledge are needed by that particular employer
  - Link your examples to evidence in your résumé
  - Customize your letter to the reader, his/her company, and the specific job
- Avoid rambling
- Reduce use or repetition of the word "I" (although using this word IS acceptable)
- Make sure to sign the letter and never Xerox a signature (unless sending it through e-mail, the Web, or fax)
  - Use GOOD PEN to sign all cover letters
    - Know what a good pen is...
  - Hit the enter key three or four times after the closing phrase (e.g., Sincerely, Kind Regards, etc.) to give space for the signature
  - Type your name underneath your signature
- Verbally highlight the most relevant/important parts of your background/experience
  - Select one or two detailed narratives for the middle of your letter rather than giving several vague concepts
  - A bulleted list of criteria is acceptable when appropriate for the job and employer
- Make sure the letter is neat (i.e., no spelling errors, grammatical errors, or typographical errors)
- Have someone else proofread and critique your letter!!!!!!!!!!!!!!!!!!

Cover Letter Directions Per Paragraph

Your Header Here
match the look of your résumé so you have one consistent look for all materials

___

Date (consider right justifying depending on style)

Employer's Name (and Position Title)
Company Name
Company Street Address
Company City, State ZIP

Note: Your cover letter look (font, style, paper, formatting, etc...) should match the look of your résumé. Do not use a template.

Do **NOT** copy the *look or layout* shown here. Use this for content information only.

Dear Mr. /Ms. /Dr. Someone,

Paragraph 1: Draw attention and make the employer want to read more. (element #1) **Make this paragraph about connecting you to the employer**. Give an example of what you know about the person or company from your research (do NOT include negative information about either). Be focused and lead to the reason why you are applying for this job (note what it is) with this company.

Paragraph 2. This paragraph is about becoming a more real and substantial person in the eyes of your potential employer. (element #2) **You should give a specific instance in which you used a skill and organize it in a S.A.R./P.A.R. format**. Explain the situation, the way that you handled it, and the positive outcome. Tell of one instance/narrative with specifics not a list of several examples. Be vivid and specific but with great word economy. Include specifics that link to your résumé. Finally, apply that instance/skill to the current company or position.

You could relate this information to something positive about their company and state why you would like to work there. Two paragraphs *could* be used instead of one but only if necessary (most should be one paragraph). This is the paragraph for your potential new employer to get an impression of you.

Paragraph 3. The last paragraph of your letter must leave a good impression with the potential employer. (element #3) **This is where you should be proactive**. Mention your enclosed résumé if you have enclosed one – or any other material. Put the ball in your court. Tell the person when YOU will follow up to make sure that all of your materials have been received or to discuss the status of your application. Don't be obnoxious and state that this conversation *will* lead to an interview or other expectation. You can in this section also thank the employer for reading your letter and considering you for the job.

Yours truly/Sincerely/Sincerely yours (or other formal ending),

(Signature – in *good* pen)
Typed Name (directly under signature)

Encl: (*if* you have enclosed a résumé, portfolio, or other relevant materials – and then state WHAT you enclosed)
Cc: (*if* you have copied/ sent the letter to someone else and then note last name(s) here)

Cover Letter Example 1

Darlene Deliuth

423 South Avenue
South Wyoming, CA 18622
AM22222@wcupa.edu
(125) 555-7422

William C. Weldon- Human Resources Director
Johnson &Johnson
P.O. Box 726, Langhorne, PA 19047-0726   September 17, 2012

Dear Mr. Weldon,

As my final year of college comes to an end, much of my time is dedicated researching the pharmaceutical industry in hopes of finding a position that fits me best. I take great responsibility in my work and could not have been more excited to learn about Ortho-McNeil. I felt a strong connection when reading,

> "We believe our first responsibility is to the doctors, nurses and patients, to mothers and fathers and all others who use our products and services. In meeting their needs everything we do must be of high quality... We are responsible to our employees, the men and women who work with us throughout the world. Everyone must be considered as an individual. We must respect their dignity and recognize their merit... We are responsible to the communities in which we live and work and to the world community as well. We must be good citizens."

This is the company with whom I would like to work and I could not have been more excited to see your opening for a Professional Skin Care Sales Representative based in Philadelphia, PA. I believe that I am the perfect candidate for your opening.

In my time at West Chester University of Pennsylvania, I have been working 45 hours a week to finance my own education. I believe that I must be responsible to my parents to take on this role as well as to myself for becoming the best student and person that I can be. Part of my work has been to have the best sales in my work as a waitress. Working as a waitress for many years as taught me the importance of independence, toughness, and how to interact with various personality types – leading to a sales of 60% over my colleagues. If your organization is seeking a truly motivated individual that will take great pride in company outcomes, I know that you should contact me.

I welcome the opportunity to discuss this position with you. My résumé is enclosed and I may be reached at contact information above. I will be in touch with you during the week of December 15, 2008 to follow up and see what other information I might provide to you. I am very excited about this opportunity and about Ortho-McNeil and I thank you for your consideration.

Sincerely,

Darlene Deliuth

Darlene Deliuth

Cover Letter Example 2

JENNIFER L. SMITH

12 South Drive
West Temple, PA 19460-9345
484.555.6987
js_smith@kanan.edu

June 11, 2014

Tierney Communications
c/o Mr. Tom Cannizzaro
200 South Broad Street
Philadelphia, PA 19102-3899

Dear Mr. Cannizzaro,

I so enjoyed our conversation in February. It was a good opportunity to catch up and I was excited to hear that Tierney is looking for new talent. As you know, I have had a long interest in and experience with Public Relations. My time as a Public Relations intern on the McDonalds Team this past summer at Tierney showed me that your reputation as one of the most prestigious organizations in the Philadelphia area was well deserved. I hope to join your organization on a more permanent basis.

Working in the Communications industry has allowed me to refine my skills working with the public. I wanted to relay to you an instance that occurred while I was working at Candy for all Occasions: A woman had placed an order two days before it was expected, and due to a miscommunication between her and another employee, her order was filled incorrectly. These circumstances put me in the difficult situation of mediating between the owner, who was on the phone, and the customer to rectify the situation by conforming to the language of each party, negotiating a resolution that would satisfy the customer's need while keeping the cost of reproduction at a minimum and saving face for the company. As a result, the situation left the customer satisfied and the order filled to her liking and me with an enlightened idea of what I would want for a career. With a background in customer service and a business background, I believe that my qualifications would be applicable in an agency setting – such as Tierney.

From my experience, I refined organizational skills, participated in planning meetings, and enhanced networking skills. These learning experiences is why I am so interested in gaining further experience through your company; I consider myself a hard- working, goal oriented, personable, resourceful worker who would like to work for a company with the same work ethic. I look forward to providing you with further details about my qualifications (in person, or via phone or e-mail). Please contact me at your earliest convenience. I will follow up with you to see what other information you may need from me during the week of June 28, 2010. Thank you for your time and consideration.

Sincerely,

Jennifer Smith

Jennifer L. Smith

Encl: Résumé & Portfolio
CC: Human Resources (Gail Drake)

Outlines and Additional Examples

Speaking Outline Example 1 (no cited research)

Mike Willis
SPK 230 – Sawyer
Page 1 of 1

Topic: learning at work/ **General Purpose**: inform
Specific Purpose: inform the audience on how learning over time impacts job success
Type of Structure: Chronological

Introduction: new job as banker / lots of difficult situations/ positive attitude

Thesis: My work experience over time provides me with opportunities to learn about myself.

1-2-3 Preview Signpost: initial training, on the job experiences, end of the year reviews

Claim One: A new job provides learning opportunities through <u>initial training</u>.
1. two week training
2. failed first test
    - studied at night
    - re-evaluate as a chance to learn (not stress)
3. highest rank in my group

Signpost/ Transition 1-2: initial training, on the job experiences

Claim Two: It is our choice to view <u>on the job experiences</u> at work as chances to learn new success strategies.
1. angry customer (over draft fee)
2. learned how to delete customer fee
3. look to me for strategies

Signpost/ Transition 2-3: on the job experiences, end of the year reviews

Claim Three: <u>End of the year reviews</u> are a positive means of learning how to improve at work.
1. bad reviews/ good reviews
2. ask for reviews (help to learn)
3. showing improvement = happy boss

1-2-3 Review Signpost: initial training, on the job experiences, end of the year reviews

Re-state Thesis: Work experience provides us with daily opportunities to learn about ourselves.
Conclusion: looking for learning over time like this with any new job

Speaking Outline Example 2 (with cited research)

Caroline Dunn
SPK 230 – Sawyer
Page 1 of 2

Topic: Randstad Human Resources Marketing Campaign
GP: Inform / SP: Randstad Marketing Strategies
Type of Structure: Categorical

Introduction:
- seeing catchy flyers in classrooms
- not use this method for Randstad

Thesis: Marketing Campaigns are the means to getting Randstad's name out without using advertising.

1-2-3 Preview Signpost: company policy, marketing campaigns, marketing strategies

Claim One: It is Randstad company policy not to use advertising.
1. company policy   (Randstad, 2005)
2. CEO rationale - be viewed as high class (Gunderbery, 2004; Grazer and Dohn, 2004)
3. other methods used by Randstad (Trotman, 1999)
4. other methods used by other companies (AP Wire, 2004)

Signpost 1-2: company policy, marketing campaigns

Claim Two: Marketing campaigns work to promote a name without using direct advertising.
1. marketing vs. advertising explanation   (Stapleton, 1990)
2. marketing methods (Grazer and Dohn, 2004; Terrance, 2001)
      - pr
      - press
      - word of mouth
      - success rates per method (Terrance, 2001)

Signpost 2-3: marketing campaigns, marketing strategies

Claim Three: Marketing strategies for this company involves using the most effective methods.
1. Public Relations with State Schools   (PASCU, 2001)
2. Job Fairs   (Donner, 2005)
          - on campus (PASCU, 2001; WCU, 2005)
          - off campus   (Kelly, 2004)
3. Club Visits (PASCU, 2001; WCU, 2005)

1-2-3 Review Signpost: company policy, marketing campaigns, marketing strategies

Re-state Thesis: Marketing Campaigns are a feasible, non-advertising method to getting Randstad's name out where you want it to be.

Conclusion:
- seeing catchy flyers in classrooms
- not use this method for Randstad
- now use marketing campaigns

References

AP Wire. (2004). Human resources has a friend: Staffing agencies take over daily HR tasks. *AP Wire*. Retrieved on April 11, 2002 from http://www.wctrib.com/event/article/id/81803/.

Donner, (2005). Finding job fairs that actually have jobs. *The Wall Street Journal*. Retrieved on April 15, 2006 from http://online.wsj.com/article/SB1000142405274870468190457 632154398884 1626.html.html.

Grazer, D. L., & Dohn, K. (2004). Your CEO strategies for confident employees. *Management Quarterly, 2,* 34-41.

Gunderbery, J (2004). A message from Jack Gunderbery: Ranstad CEO. *Randstad Staffing Agency*. Retrieved on April 11, 2006 from http://www.randstadusa.com/about-randstad/leadership.

Kelly, D. (2004). *201 strategies to get your company name out*. Philadelphia, PA: Fountain Head Press.

PASCU. (2001). Inter-campus association affiliations in our state schools. *PASCUA*. Retrieved on April 15, 2006 from http://www.PASCU.org/ article/id/287798/.

Randstad. (2005). About Randstad. *Randstad Staffing Agency*. Retrieved on April 11, 2006 from http://www.randstadusa.com/about-randstad.

Stapleton, J. (1990). Marketing vs. advertising in plain language. *Marketing Today, 11,* 6-13. Retrieved on April 10, 2006 from Academic Search Premiere database.

Terrance, K. S. (2001). Marketing strategies in a mediated age. *The American Marketing Association of America*. Retrieved April 11, 2006, from: http://www.ldonline.org/ ld_indepth/speech-language/lda_milestones.html.

Trotman, J. (1999, March 12). Staffing agencies are pulling out all the stops for business. *The Wall Street Journal,* p. D1.

Speaking Outline Example 3 (persuasive example with cites)

Topic: MAC vs. PC corporate use
GP: Persuade / SP: Show how MAC is more positive in a comparison to PCs
Type of Structure: Compare & Contrast

Introduction:
- initial training at company
- Dell: lost files; difficulty in navigation for new employees
- 4 year outcome for Mac (PC Magazine, 2012)

Thesis: Computer use in our company must be about making hard choices between Macintosh and PC.

C/C Preview Signpost: Using a PC, Using a Mac

Claim One: Using a PC at our company has very specific utility.
1. Positive Elements
      a. Low Cost (Eigen, 2011; Tech Notes, 2012)
      b. Custom built (Dreg, 2011)
      c. Compatibility with hardware - some (Harvard Business Review, 2011)
2. Negative Elements
      a. Longevity Issues (Derrli & Goades, 2012; Eigen, 2011)
      b. Security problems (Abe, 2011; NYT – Schnet, 2012; Time editors, 2012)
      c. Cost to customize (NYT – Schnet, 2013)
      d. Compatibility with hardware - ONLY some (Harvard Business Review, 2011)

Signpost/ Transition: PC, Mac

Claim Two: Using a Mac at our company may have more developed utility for our needs.
1. Negative Elements
      a. High Cost (Eigen, 2011; Tech Notes, 2012)
      b. Low customization (Farrell, 2013)
2. Positive Elements
      a. Good Security (Abe, 2011; Balin, 2013; NYT – Schnet, 2012; Time editors, 2012)
      b. Longevity (Derrli & Goades, 2012; Eigen, 2011)
      c. High compatibility (Bart, 2012; Harvard Business Review, 2011)
      d. Quality of Software (Tech Notes, 2012)
      e. Ease of navigation – company survey (unpublished data, 2015)

1-2-3 Review Signpost: Using a PC, Using a Mac

Re-state Thesis: Computer use in our company leads us to make the choices to use Macintosh over the PC options.

Conclusion:
- Dell: lost files; difficulty in navigation for new employees
- initial training at company – turn this around
- 4 year outcome for our company (personal communication, Janet Deitz, CEO)

Agenda Example

Political Communication Group Annual Meeting
When: August 17, 2014
Where: Riverfront Room / **Time:** 9:00am-11:00am

Officers/ Meeting Organizers
- Immediate Past Chair: **Theodore Schekels**, Randolph- Macon College
- Chair: **J. Kanan Sawyer**, West Chester University
- Vice Chair: **Jason Edwards**, Bridgewater State University
- Secretary: **Janis Edwards**, University of Alabama

Old Business (**Kanan Sawyer**) 45 minutes
- Approval of 2011 Meeting Notes
- Carry-Over Issues
   o No-Shows
   o Coffee (vs. Wine) and Spots
- Submission and Acceptance Information
   o numbers
   o matching reviewers (*please sign up to review or chair*)

Reports
- Executive Council (**Lisa Gring-Pemble**) 15 minutes
- Planners' Meeting Information (**Jason Edwards**) 10 minutes

New Business
- Planning for 2015 (**Jason Edwards**) 35 minutes
   o notes from the planners' meeting
   o need for a change in the call?
- Elections (**Kanan Sawyer**) 15 minutes
   o **Political Communication Executive Council Rep**: elected this year but no meeting attendance required; begins attendance for 3 year term in 2014
   o **Secretary**: 4 year commitment that moves through the position levels

Brief Overview of Positions
- **Secretary**: major responsibility is Wine & Spots (collect videos, put together presentation, work with ECA planners on room reservations and food and beverage details, *get funding for the event*, advertise the event, arrange for all necessary technology, prepare a discussion outline to facilitate the "spots"), take notes at the business meeting and send to members
- **Vice-Chair**: attend planners' meeting, meet with chair at convention to transfer information and materials
- **Chair**: plan all aspects of the convention (send out the program call, collect all submissions, recruit qualified reviewers,
- **Immediate Past Chair**: serve in an advisory capacity to the chair and assist with any overflow details with program planning or communication

Next Meeting: August 17, 2015 (time and location tba)

Part C:

PowerPoint Reality

Taken from *PowerPoint ® Reality: Slides in Real Audiences with Real Easy Steps* by J. Kanan Sawyer

The standards in this section are to be used for all PowerPoint slides shows used in SPK 230 for group or individual presentations and the evaluation in this course packet reflects those standards.

TABLE OF CONTENTS

A DIFFERENT LENS

IN THE BOOK/ NOT IN THE BOOK/ WHY THIS BOOK?...

As you may have guessed, not every speech needs visual support, and those speeches that do may not need PowerPoint™ support. If your speech does not, well, you shouldn't have purchased this book and shouldn't go through this process. However, if you do need visual support for your talk, PowerPoint slides can be an amazing way to help your audience visually picture (redundant, right?) what you have to say.

PowerPoint slides are an incredible tool for showing visual information to a large audience, helping to guide an audience along the structure of a speech, adding visual movement to a talk, helping your audience to follow and recall your ideas, and even professionally presenting small amounts of text.

If you have chosen to use slides – let's not fall into the trap of creating slides that make our audience cringe. Sadly, most slides do. With so many PowerPoint help guides on the market, why is it that we are still seeing... this?!?!!?

Good question. I have used any number of PowerPoint textbooks in my career and, as a professor, I have assigned any number of them to my students. What I found myself doing was supplementing these books with some very foundational

Marketability for Career success

- Skills & Experience gained
  - Confidence Building is crucial to showing socials skills in networking
  - Team Building will become a neccesary part of any job or project
  - Building Character will help to make you a more marketable property
  - Time Management Skills will open up more options for you
  - Be both Honest & Responsible

information – from a *communication theory* perspective. EEK. Before you put this book down because in the first page it used the word "theory," consider instead that what you heard was this:

PowerPoint presentations are failing because they have missed the mark of effectively *communicating* with their audiences.

There is an entire discipline of Communication Studies that has grown since Greek times and instructs its followers that messages must be centered on the "audience" in order to have an impact. If messages are distracting or disconnected, well, then you can kiss your impact goodbye. So, where is the connection with PowerPoint???

It seems that most PowerPoint books fall into two categories: 1) "How To" do everything books, and 2) design books. This book is a little of both but also what you will find here is a look at PowerPoint through a different lens – as a means to link your audience to you and vice versa. You will hear the word audience **a lot** throughout this text.

MAKING IT EASY

It is rare that I speak to a group that has no PowerPoint experience (if that is you, don't panic, we can get you through). Some folks have started with mandatory PowerPoint assignments in *elementary* school! Most people have had to put together a presentation for something or another… and everyone seems to have seen a slide show.

So, if you have no experience in opening a slide or putting text on a slide then you may should know that you may need a "How To" manual or an online tutorial at some point to learn the basics (consider: http://www.actden.com/pp2007/index.htm - it's like the Dick and Jane of tutorials). If, however, you have those two criteria down – or feel comfortable doing a quick internet search (e.g., "insert text in PowerPoint") – then you have the skill set to make this book a valuable tool, which will provide you with the following:

- a simple means of connecting you to your audience
- step by step instructions for creating audience-centered templates
- tools for altering images *without* the need of other software
- a clear understanding of how slides work *with* your speech
- comfortable delivery techniques that will differentiate you from other presenters
- and (of course) a few tricks

My goal is to provide you with steps in a simple format that will eliminate anxiety and keep PowerPoint from being a big time-suck in your life. While the images in this book are specific to PC users, the design concepts apply to MAC users, as do many of the short cuts, which are in both "languages."

Sound good? (And, now that "theory" word is a bit less jarring.)

CRITICS, OPPONENTS, DETRACTORS – WHAT'S UP WITH THAT?

Before we launch into making your life easier when working with PowerPoint, we need to take a quick moment to address the common criticisms of the medium so that you will not fall into these traps.

If you have seen a PowerPoint show then you have probably seen at least some bad PowerPoint. In fact, one author even claims not only that PowerPoint is evil, but that, "*Power corrupts. PowerPoint corrupts absolutely*" (tee hee hee) (This is from Edward Tufte's, 2003 article in Wired Magazine, in case you're looking!)

The arguments against PowerPoint contend that slides:
- have poor visual quality
- limit content
- disconnect speakers and audiences

Marketability for Career success

- Skills & Experience gained
  - Confidence Building is crucial to showing socials skills in networking
  - Team Building will become a neccesary part of any job or project
  - Building Character will help to make you a more marketable property
  - Time Management Skills will open up more options for you
  - Be both Honest & Responsible

Yup. Totally right. No argument here. Ah… but this is because PowerPoint is being used in a way that does all of these things. If we redesign our slides, use them as *aids* to talks rather than to be the talk itself, and don't use them when they distract or are not necessary,… then we can agree with the critics and still be effective. Let's do that!

How? Like this…

You'll note that the arrangement of this book starts with a section on *Audience*, which is followed by an *Organizing* section containing discussions of both text and images (typically the bulk of "how-to" manuscripts), and lastly, some *Adding* and *Presenting*. As you read along, your attention will be shifted from what you can do with PowerPoint to what you ought to do in order to connect and change your audiences. The result will be a presentation unlike that of any of your colleagues. Your presentation will be remembered because your audience will finally know that you are talking *to them*!

So, what you get here is a bit different. This book is an attempt to shift your focus. It is an attempt to help you *connect* to your audience. Read on… and you will find yourself having a few "Ah Ha!" and "Reeeealllly???!" moments that change your PowerPoint slides (and your presentations) forever.

Enjoy.

AUDIENCE

"TO... NOT FROM"

Why is *audience* the thing that most PowerPoint books have failed to address? Communication scholars will tell you that this is the foundation of our public address. Yet suddenly it's all about us? Where is the "audience" in PowerPoint?

For example, who is the audience for *this* (actual slide)?!?!

If you were on the receiving end of this slide show presentation, would you be captivated? Engaged? Appreciative of how your speaker knew you – or took the time to target the speech just to you? Probably not. More likely, you would be thinking... "huh?"

Before we criticize, let us reflect on two important considerations. First, it is likely that each of us has constructed equally as dissociative slides. Second, audiences change. We may give the same speech of the same topic to several different groups and, yet, have constructed only one set of slides. Even more out of our control, many employees are at the mercy of their employers who use stock slide templates for <u>all</u> of their presentations.

Unfortunately, these have become our excuses. These are the pitfalls of *habitual slide creation*. Hearken back to the days of your college public speaking class (or, perhaps you are in such a class now or side stepped this all-important course). Your professor would have instructed you to make every speech be about, for, and to the very audience in front of you. Sure, the topic, format, and even much of your evidence may be the same, but if you did not relate your stories, examples, language, and style to your specific listeners, then you would have failed to meet a very basic communication principle. (Aristotle would be distraught!)

Speeches and slides must be "audience-centered." However, for as basic a foundation as this may sound, consider the slide right here. *Who* is the audience?

Is it for mothers-to-be, hospital care workers, or nursing students? Is it a little disconnected?

GOOD PRENATAL CARE IS..

• NO CIGARETTE SMOKING

• NO ALCOHOL AND DRUG USE

• LOW EXPOSURE TO TERATOGENS

• AVOID EXCESSIVE PHYSICAL WORK

Let's fix it!!

This new version of the same information helps to clarify our all-important audience! See?? The information is the same. The speaker is the same. Yet the visual elements are very easily manipulated to be about a *specific* audience. In this case, the audience is the King County Prenatal Care System and the speaker is the company Nurses Training, Inc.

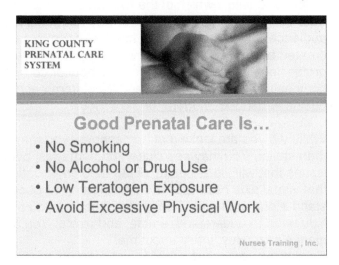

The images and the layout can be grabbed right off the audience's website! (Read on for laws from the Fair Use Act on image grabbing as well as text versus visual focus!)

Some readers, at this point, will be panicked. Every audience?!? Every speech?! Who has the time? This is where template construction is your friend.

TEMPLATE CONSTRUCTION

Templates are not backgrounds. Backgrounds are the colors behind your words or visuals. Templates are the designs that make up the tone, format (or organization), and layout of your entire PowerPoint show.

Microsoft offers you several templates or "Design Themes" along with their software.

Some of these templates are as old as time. Office 2007 has updated many of the Microsoft designs to be more visually appealing than in previous versions. That's great – except for one thing. As good looking as they are... Microsoft still doesn't know who <u>your</u> audience is.

No matter how much you think that your slides are pretty or captivating (or even shocking!), **unaltered Microsoft PowerPoint templates will never be about or for your specific audience.**

There are two solutions:
- design your own templates
- manipulate given designs

AUDIENCE FEEL

Before you select which of the two options of template construction you will use, you must get a "feel" for your audience. The best way to do this is to simply look at the materials put out by your audience, which are designed for this very purpose – such as a company website. Websites are created by companies to be a visual representation of that organization's tenor and professionalism. Look at your own school or company's website. Compare that to its direct competitors. Do you get a different feel from each of them? Is one more friendly, inviting, playful, business-minded, modern, or old school?

While we you are looking at homepages, you may find that some websites' visual appeal is less than stellar. You may see clutter, poor images, overuse of text, too many types of fonts, or other issues that will violate many of the recommendations laid out in this manual. Remember, first, that visual aids have a different purpose (i.e., supporting a speech) than do websites, which are stand-alone mediums. Remember, second, you aren't supposed to copy... that's plagiarism. ☺ You need to understand, emote, and relate. You are supposed to have your audience upon first glance say, "Hey, that's about me!"
So, take a peek. Get a feel – and read on to determine your next step!

> **Note**: If your group has no website, no worries. Look at brochures, letterhead, graphic designs, and sales materials – even office décor! Get a feel about your group from the materials that they send out as representations of who they are. Remember that if your group *does* have a website, they will update often and you should always be checking back for style and image changes.

LET'S TAKE A MOMENT TO DISCUSS LEGALITY.

Unless you designed the background or logo, unless you took the picture, unless you created the company-specific color (like Tiffany blue or Coca Cola red), then you must have _written permission to_ use these elements. If you do not, it's stealing! (Don't steal.)

It is difficult to find the details for penalties related to image poaching. Below is a brief overview (further details may be found many places, including:
http://www.buscalegis.ufsc.br/revistas/index.php /buscalegis/article/viewFile/3450/3021, which is the source for some of this information):

The penalties for copying images, audio, or others' materials without permission include:
- Fines up to the actual amount of damages
- Statutory damages up to $100,000 *per* infringement
- Criminal penalties of up to one year in jail and fines up to $25,000

You may notice that many of your professors do or have used others' images or logos. This is often (but not always) permitted under the protection of "fair use." Fair Use refers to the copyright standards that allow individuals to copy others' work for "purposes such as...

teaching, scholarship, or research…" without requiring author permission. That being said, the copyright guidelines further clarify that educators or those in an educational setting cannot just take what they want and use it. This means that "fair use" has limits, which is why even teachers are limited to 5 images per author and no more than 10% of a text or 1,000 words. If an educator violates this standard, "depending on the circumstances, educators may not be required to pay statutory damages (as high as $150,000 per instance), but they may still have to pay copyright owners actual damages caused by their *illegal* copying, plus legal fees."

Therefore, if you choose to use others' images, **you must pay for usage** as dictated by the author and be sure to cite: author's name, title of work – and it is from the internet, name of site, date posted and/ or revised, date obtained, and URL. If you select an image but drastically alter it such that it is "distinctly different from the original," your work would not be considered "poaching."

If your co-workers or friends are using the ole "copying what I wanna" method and are not covered under the Fair Use provisions or do not have written permission from the image or text owners then those folks (or you) are in fact breaking the law. If you use these elements in the classroom as part of learning, then you have permission to do so. If you, however, use these classroom created slides as part of a portfolio or as examples of your work that you show outside the classroom then you are NOT covered under Fair Use and you are subject to the full penalty of the law.

(Good to know, huh!?!)

To Cite or Not To Cite… Should Never Be a Question.

If you have developed a strong speech grounded on research, you want your audience to know! Speeches are a time to flaunt your credibility but putting together cumbersome references in a visual medium can create a quandary. To simply paste up a list of references in a final slide would violate many of our rules of text design (read on). Not to reference them at all would violate legal and ethical standards. The choice of how to cite your sources, however, is up to you. How should you reference your contributing sources without cluttering your slides??

First, consider again that PowerPoint is a visual medium. Blocks of text are better suited to handouts and your audience may indeed wish to have a take-home list of your sources. If so, present your sources in that medium.

Second, you may want your audience to see your sources as they come up in your talk and, thus, listing names on each slide per bullet could be the most clear communication method – just keep your text amount minimal.

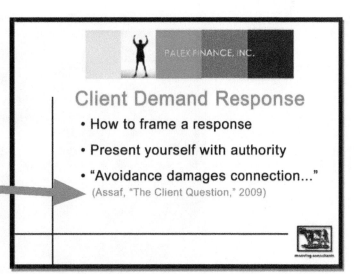

"3 out of 4 presentations, according to John Zagger of the New York Times, use distracting PowerPoint slides!"

Third, remember that your slides will aid a verbal presentation and simply stating your sources out loud is always the best way to "show" your credibility!

Whatever you decide, keep your references in sync with the look, feel, and good design rules of your PowerPoint slides – and remember that citations should be announced or visible for anything that you have taken from another source.

Charts

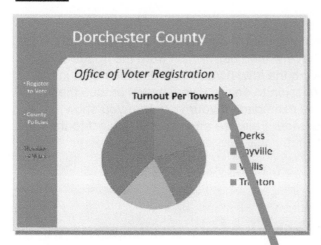

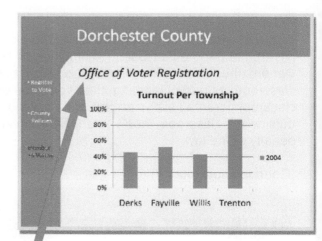

Cites

Images

Lynn Sawyer, Sawyer Photography 2010

DESIGN YOUR OWN TEMPLATES

Designing your own PowerPoint templates is far easier than you may have guessed. Those with lots of PowerPoint skill can get super fancy but even those with the most basic knowledge can design audience-centered templates that grab viewers!

Design is about shape and placement. Audience-centered templates are about color and tone. Once you have "researched" the look of your group, set up slides that demonstrate an understanding and keen attention to their tone, font, colors, and (with permission from your audience or under Fair Use guidelines) the layout.

For instance, if you were part of the "XMS Green Marketing" group and giving a talk to Kelson's Gourmet grocery, you would take a peek at Kelson's **current website...**

... and could create a show using any of the following four looks:

Note: Each template uses elements of the existing website but that four different looks are developed – each of which effectively links to the audience.

Look Number One

The first look (because we have permission of the audience!) literally mimics the look of the webpage – including images and layout. Next, it mimics the background color of the website and pastes a box of that color over the website text to create a space for new words! (If you cannot find the specific color in the PowerPoint "format background" standard colors, you can actually copy the webpage and crop down to create color boxes. (See the instructions later in this section).

The next two looks also clearly link to the audience by copying specific elements of the webpage.

Look Number Two

Look Two uses the same font type as well as the audience's logo and pictures with a very simple and basic background (removing elements can keep the audience feel but help to limit clutter on your slides).

Look Number Three

Look Three uses the logo and font type but mimics the background of some of the photos rather than using specific images!

Look Number Four

Look Four keeps it basic. For folks who are worried that excessive creativity is needed to connect to your audience, stop worrying!

This looks simply changes the colors on a Microsoft template and add the company logo. No frills– but still connects!

Time to Create??

So many options. So little time!
Yes, time. How (you may ask) difficult is this process and how much time will it take?

Those new to creating their own slides can be trepidacious about the effort involved in putting these together. Relax.

This guide is designed to make the steps easy – and we start in the very next section.

STEPS TO CREATING A SLIDE TEMPLATE

Step 1: Mimic Background Color or Copy Background Elements

Embrace your right click. Most slide elements can be copied (remember... with permission or under the Fair Use guidelines – this cannot be stressed enough!!!) by simply putting your cursor on the element that you desire to have on your slide, right clicking and copying – then pasting onto your slides. Easy!

MAC vs. PC Note:
Right click?! If you are a MAC person, you may be feeling left out at this notation and laughing that another computer guide has fallen prey to the swift grasp of the PC fad.

Not to worry, in this text you will find shortcut methods in both PC and MAC language and, where they have been unwittingly omitted, remember that these steps are typically easy to find with a quick search on the internet!

(ps... control click on a MAC is the same as right click on a PC) ☺

As you go about selecting and pasting, you will see that some elements will paste beautifully, some will come up in pieces (bummer – lots of right clicking) and if you want more than just a single element... lots and lots of right clicking. Watch out for carpal tunnel!

Alternatively, consider the use of "**Ctrl-Alt-PrtSc**" – or a "Print Screen" / Screen Capture copy method, which will capture whatever you are showing on your desktop. You can then paste the element onto your slide ("**Ctrl + V**") and crop out unwanted elements or paste over them. (MAC users can do the same function with "**Command-Control-Shift-3**," which also places the image onto your clipboard so it can then be pasted into a slide.)

For example, if you go to the Kelson website, select "Ctrl + Alt + Prt Sc," and then paste (right click or "Ctrl + V") it onto a blank slide, you will get:

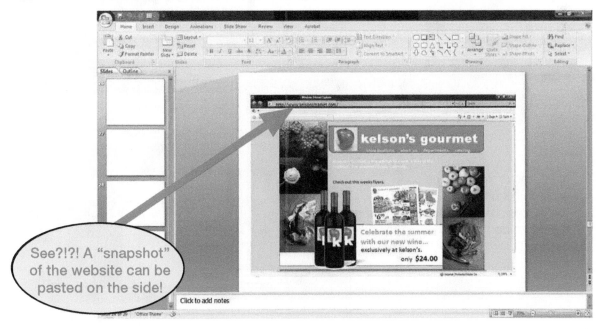

See?!?! A "snapshot" of the website can be pasted on the side!

Step 2: Add a Space for Text or Images

As you might note from the example above, some website "backgrounds" are not a suitable basis for layering on your text or images. This one is FULL of advertisements and excess images. If you tried to add your own stuff to this, the slide would be busy and cluttered.

In other instances, the background may be complex and make your text hard to see or be distracting to the eye. YOU NEED SPACE!!

How do you get that space? Add some boxes! It's that simple. Background color-matched boxes or other shapes placed on top of unnecessary elements will add areas on the slide for *your* words and images. It's like painting over the middle of a canvas.

Here's how:
1. Go to the "Insert" Tab and select your shape (in this case, it's a square but you may need a circle or some other shape to hide what you don't want & leave what you do).

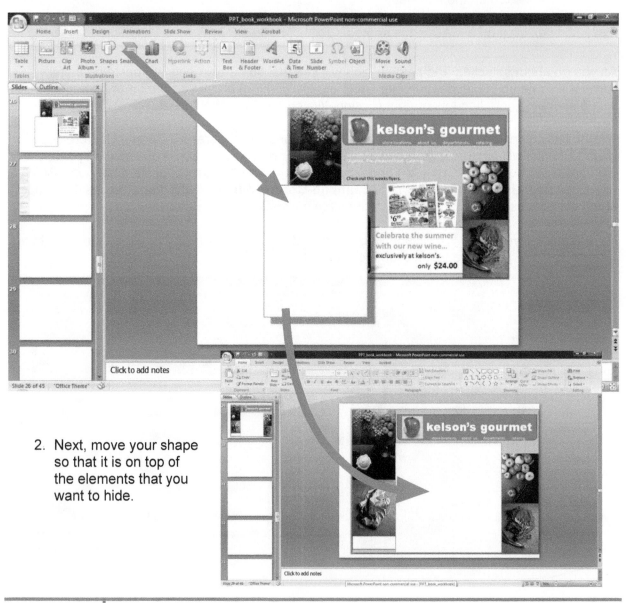

2. Next, move your shape so that it is on top of the elements that you want to hide.

3. Be sure to change the shape so that it matches the <u>background color</u> of your slide.

Now you have a clean canvas! If you would like even more room for your own information or images, just place another color-matched shape over more images until you get the perfect blend of room for you and look from them.

Creating That Perfect Color Match

Most colors are created by right clicking and selecting "format background." From this spot, you can alter from limitless possibilities. (MAC users can also select the shape and then open the Toolbox to the Formatting Palette and select "Colors, Weights, and Fills.")

However, what if you cannot find your chosen background color and your created colors just seem a bit off? Do not fret. Use your "Ctrl + Alt + Prt Sc" function again to copy the website and simply crop down to just a color section of your desired background color.

Next, you can make this box bigger or copy the one box and paste it EVERYWHERE that you want a blank spot! This is an automatic exact color match! (See the Visuals section to learn how to "Crop.")

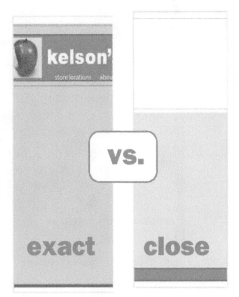

Step 3: Layer With Key Images, Terms, Or Other "Template" Elements

Once you have a nice canvas, you can start placing your additional elements. You can add text, pictures, or even bullets that are specific to the audience.

Bullets that are specific to the audience? Huh? How can such little dashes capture my specific audience? **Bullets CAN be more than just dots and dashes!** If you are hoping to make your slides just that extra bit more specified, try adding an image as a bullet, perhaps your company's logo or a picture!?!

The key is to always make sure that these are large enough to see as tiny little bullets and do not clutter the slide. How?? Simple! Follow these steps:

1. Highlight the words that you would like to have with bullets.
2. Go to the "Home" Tab.
3. Click on the <u>arrow down</u> next to the bullets button.

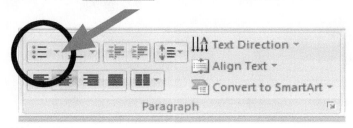

4. Select the "Bullets and Numbering" option.

5. Select "Picture."

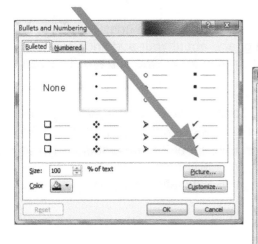

fyi: the "Pictures" you will see are stock images. ew...
Most of these are pretty boring (e.g., a red box).

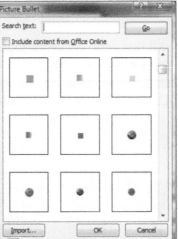

6. Click to "Import" and select from any image saved on your computer – including any images saved from internet searches or a homepage (remember image copyright! ☺).

7. Select "Add" – NOT "Add To" – and your image will appear as an option.

8. Click to add your option and it will appear!

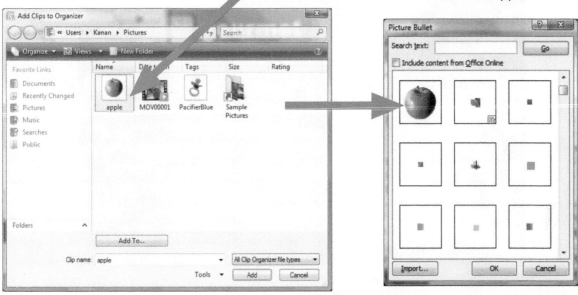

TRA LA!!!!

Your bullet will appear! If it is too **BIG** or too tiny, go back to the first screen and play with the image size with "size"/ % of text." Fun, huh!?!?! (And, totally audience-centered).

kelson's gourmet

store locations.   about us.   departments.   catering.

🔘 Subpoint

🔘 Subpoint

🔘 Subpoint

🔘 Subpoint

Step 4: Include an Author Identifying Element (as needed)

As you are wrapping up the final steps to creating your templates, you should consider one last element. You. Primary visual cues in your slides should be <u>of and about your audience</u> but this does not mean that those folks wouldn't benefit from a visual reminder of who *you* are. This can happen in a few ways.

First, you may decide to have your name on an initial slide. Second, you may choose to have it on all subsequent slides (e.g., *XMS Green Marketing*). Third, you may elect to have some visual element such as a logo from your group or company appear throughout the presentation. These elements are ***not*** necessary but can provide a link between you and "them." This also means that you do not need to ditch all aspects your company-designed templates (just change the focus).

Step 5: Add Your Content

OK. Templates are made. Now is the time that you add your content. Do not add content until your templates and verbal presentation are complete. This will keep you focused and your organization clear. As shown before, once you have both elements complete, finishing your slides is just a matter of placing your talk onto your templates.

After some pasting…finished!!! And this section included some tricky stuff!

(For guidelines about how much text you should include, image placement, and even what kind of text/ font to use – read on to Organization and Adding!)

MANIPULATE GIVEN DESIGNS

You may not be a whiz at creating PowerPoint elements or you just may not want to go through the process. You may have a stock presentation that every person in your company must use with every single client. Again, no worries. A few minor adjustments or additions to your stock templates or Microsoft "Design Themes" can still link you to your audience.

Design Themes are found in the "Design" Tab and show little pictures of *looks* for your slides.

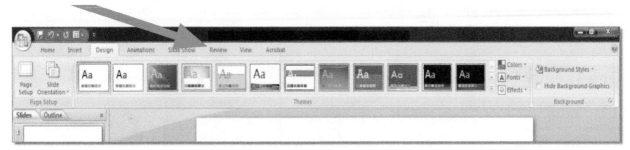

MAC users will want to use the tabs shown above each slide and select "Slide Themes."

Step 1: Select a Theme that Best Matches Your Audience.

Yes, this is still important! (In fact, it's the point). Go through each of the looks and see what has a layout or even coloring that seems to best fit your audience. These don't have to be perfect – how could they be? – but you want to start with the design that asks the least amount of work from you.

Remember these?

Select the one with the best fit!

Step 2: Alter Colors and Layer to Clarify Audience Link

Again … those Microsoft folks don't know your audience. None of these themes will have a direct link to the group with whom *you* are speaking. Now is the time for some simple alterations.

Decide what basic changes will help to best create visual links to your audience. Will it be a change of background color? Do you need to alter the font of the text? Could you realign the text from left justified to centered – or vice versa?

Any other these elements can be used to mimic the feel and/ or tone of your audience. None should take more than a few seconds but do make sure to give yourself enough time to play with color choices (see below).

For example, consider this Design Theme with two different looks (all created by only changes of color, font, or adding a circle!)

One Theme/ Two Manipulations

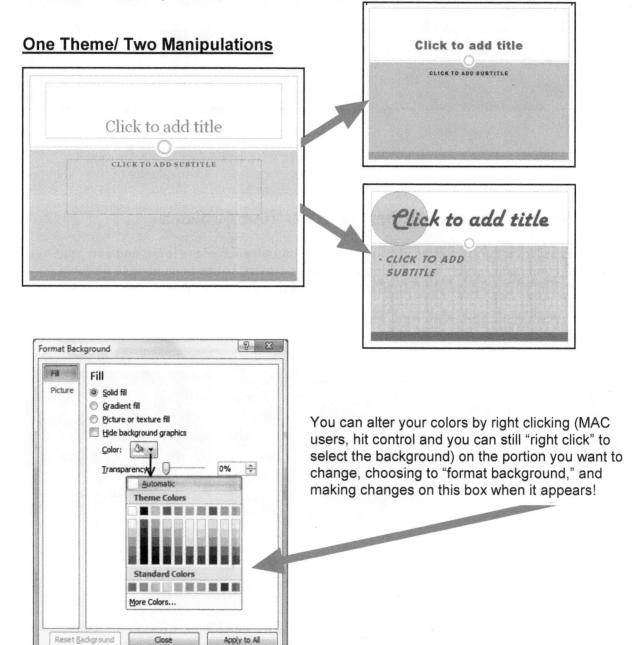

You can alter your colors by right clicking (MAC users, hit control and you can still "right click" to select the background) on the portion you want to change, choosing to "format background," and making changes on this box when it appears!

Just like above, once you have a nice canvas, you can start adding additional elements. Using the example shown earlier, you can see how simple manipulation serves as the foundation for your slide and the next steps help to complete it.

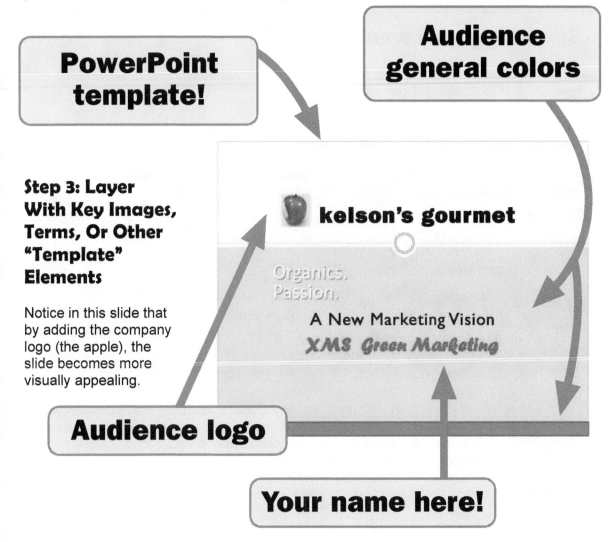

Step 3: Layer With Key Images, Terms, Or Other "Template" Elements

Notice in this slide that by adding the company logo (the apple), the slide becomes more visually appealing.

Step 4: Include an Author Identifying Element (as needed)

You may not feel the need for your name or your company name on your slides but if you do decide to include it, be sure that it is easy to read and added in a spot that does not clash with the look or layout of your other slide elements.

You may simply include your name on the first slide (part of your introduction or as a backdrop to your talk as you begin) or can include your name on all slides. Be sure that you name or company name does not overshadow the focus on your audience!

Step 5: Add Your Content...

Follow the steps from the coming sections of this text to complete the look of your slides and to finalize your visual presentation!

NOTE: *Some things just aren't pretty.*

Let's say that you have done it all (researched the look of the company, created slides that clearly resemble that look, etc...). Now, step back.

How does it look? Sometimes even when you have all the individual elements – not everything comes together. Maybe it's even, er, ...ugly.

 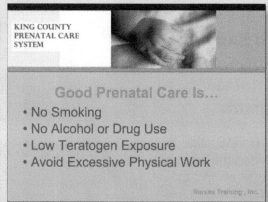

Do NOT stop editing slides after you have connected to the audience. They may still need work. Perhaps all of the elements looked fine on their website (or... didn't. Not all websites are visually ideal. Nothing you can do about that) but this look just doesn't work on the slides. Take a minute to adjust your "overall" before moving on to changing colors or deleting elements.

You can keep the *feel* and ditch the reaction of, "*yikes... what is that!?*"

Repeated Use Templates

Company Slides

If your boss insists that you use company templates, you may have little control over what elements cannot be removed from your slides. You can, however, still focus on the overall look and appeal of the slide.

Standard corporate templates can be modified in the very same way that basic Microsoft templates can be altered. Add images, change colors, include audience logos, and show that as much as you are advertising yourself, you are all about them!

Company Template

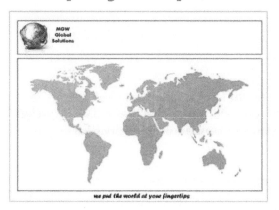

Linked to Audience

The Same Audience Over and Over Again

Another issue with slide templates is showing one audience the same templates over and over again. As important as it is to be consistent, it is just as important to let your audience know that your presentation was prepared just for them… and just for this talk! If you have had (or been) that teacher who is still using the same transparencies from 1971 – or the same slides since the 1980s (yeah… did you know that PowerPoint has been around for 20 years?!) then you know that slides can disconnect you from your audience just by appearing tired or overused.

There is no one template for a particular audience. To be effective, you need only to show a visual connection – but those visual elements can change per talk. For instance:

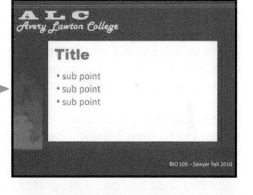

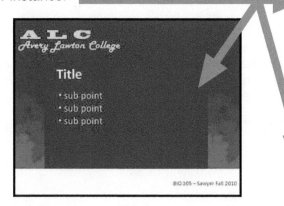

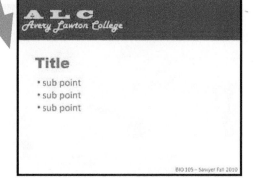

Avoid drastic changes for every talk (these are REALLY basic ☺). It is important not to appear to be scattered!

Now that your templates are complete, they can be used as the building blocks to <u>organizing</u> your audience-centered slides!

ORGANIZATION

OUTLINES

Nothing is worse than a speaker who exclaims, "But, I spent forever on my slides!" Uh oh. Bad choice. Spend forever on your *speech* and your slides will naturally reveal themselves (really!). All you will need to do is create visuals that can help your audience to: 1) **follow** your presentation and 2) **recall** your presentation.

How does one make slides soooo easily? Look to the outline of your speech.

SPEECH TO VISUAL AID LINK

Slides are like speeches. They have an introduction, a body, and a conclusion. These elements should match your verbal presentation; after all, the visuals only <u>aid your talk</u>. Aristotle would recommend that you think about your logos (that's a fancy old Greek word for *arguments*). Do! Use the outline that you have already put together for your speech to direct the text (don't just cut and paste your outline; you'll need to edit first) and select images for your slides as a means of "showing" your arguments. (hint hint… you should put together your speech *first*).

HOW MANY SLIDES???

There is no magic number on how many slides you should have per minute. Speakers often want to know… "how many slides are required?" Sorry. There is no precise answer to this. Some skilled PowerPoint users can do in two slides what may take others thirty-two to complete. This is a matter of animation use and creative layouts. Don't get caught up in the question of, "how many?" – instead think about what in your talk needs visual support.

Your visuals should coincide with your talk. If you are struggling to make your verbal… visual, remember to keep it basic. Start with the needed elements: an intro slide, a preview slide, one slide per main point, a review slide, and a conclusion slide. Add slides for subpoints as needed. Begin your construction by creating one audience-centered slide (as described above) and then *copy that slide* and *paste several of them* into the presentation.

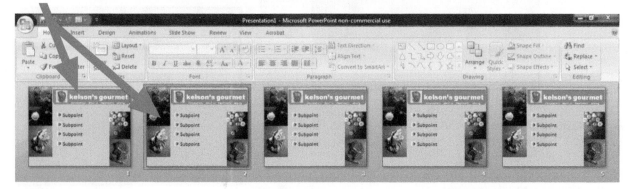

(Don't re-create it time and time again! Recreations can cause "bouncing" or slight shifts in location when shown that make the words and images appear to "bounce" up and down.)

Next, alter the slides so that they clearly link to the outline. Here's how that would look *per slide*:

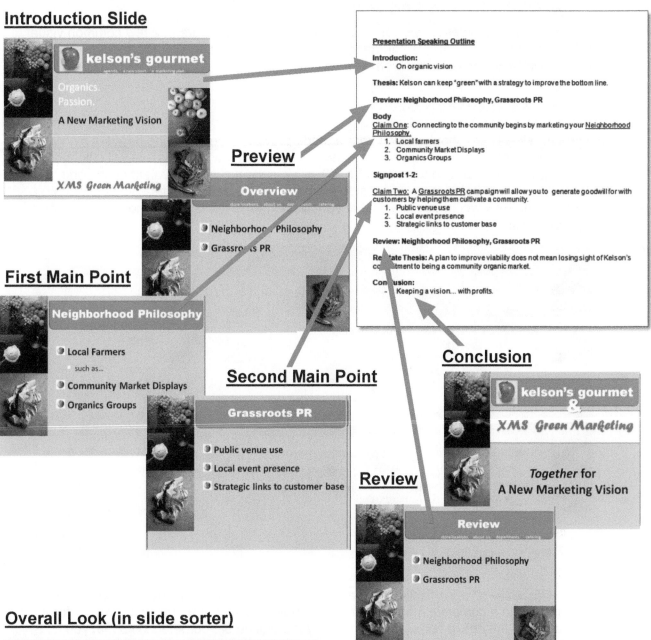

Overall Look (in slide sorter)

Go to the **Texting Section** below for guidelines on font size, type, and number of words. Go to the **Images Section** to determine how to follow the logos/ organization of your speech outline if you choose not to use or to limit your text.

COMMON VISUAL OUTLINING ERRORS

While matching your slides to your outline, it is important to be aware of a few common visual outlining errors that can lead your audience astray. Hopefully, you have heard many of these before but will heed an additional word of caution.

EEK... MISLEADING HEADINGS

Headers (or slide titles) should match your agenda/preview slide. Creating headers by using subpoints or details is like telling your audience, "In the next few minutes, we will talk about "A, B, C" and then proceeding to talk about " h, #3, iii". It is the writing equivalent of creating a Table of Contents with one set of terms but inside the book having each chapter title be something totally different. How would you know what chapter you were in? It's even more difficult when the audience can't flip back.

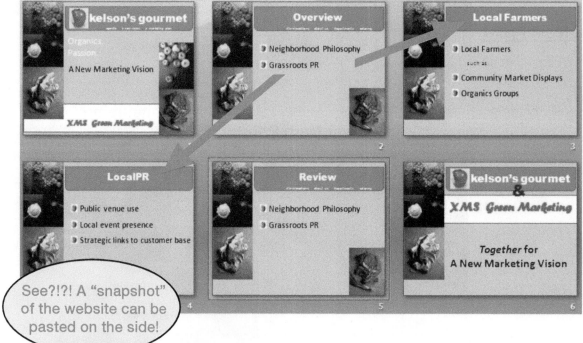

See?!?! A "snapshot" of the website can be pasted on the side!

While you may know where you are and what's up, your listeners are going through a complete mental exercise. You are insisting that they not tune out for a second and that they have committed to memory the outline of your speech so that you can elaborate on the details and they won't be lost as to where you are. AUDIENCES GET LOST. Help them out. Always make sure that the only headers that you use are the exact same words that you verbally/ visually previewed (e.g., see the presentation on page 25. Notice how all the headers are pulled off Slide #2 – word for word).

EEK... THE FIRST SLIDE GIVES IT AWAY

The first slide of your presentation *should* pull the audience into your talk. However, too many speakers will put the end of their talk (the "ask" or the conclusion) on that initial slide – allowing audiences to tune out or create barriers. This is especially problematic if your presentation is persuasive in any way.

If your first slide to a group of nurses for a presentation about how to discuss nutrition with pregnant women states, "Unhealthy Babies: You MUST Tell Your Patients To Eat Right!" – you might be in trouble. You have not yet convinced your audience of either the problems or your particular solution…. Eek! Your audience will begin creating all sorts of counter arguments or alternative choices in their heads from the start.

NO

EEK… NEGLECTING THE NEED FOR A THEME

Have you ever entered someone's house and knew that the entire thing was decorated out of Pottery Barn? Or IKEA? This is a theme. It is a look. However, what happens when you walk into one room and see IKEA, the next room screams Shabby Chic, and the next is early fraternity throw back? Things just seem off. This happens far too often in PowerPoint.

Instead, remember to link to your *verbal introduction* with the first visual slide. If you plan to begin talking about how nurses have vital conversations with their patients and then give an example of one woman that you talked to…

…then a revised slide might read, "Unhealthy Babies? What Should We Discuss With Our Patients?" This type of title grabs but doesn't give it all away!

Better!

Lack of theme is typically an issue of changing looks, varied layout, poor consistency, and forgetting the audience.

The result? Clutter, confusion, and distraction.

EEK... LAYOUT IS RANDOM FROM SLIDE TO SLIDE

If you have created an audience-centered template and then copied it to create a canvas for your slides, you should have one look. Yet even then, some things will still create a disconnect. To avoid this, K.I.S.S. (keep it simple students... yeah, that last word can have many interpretations):

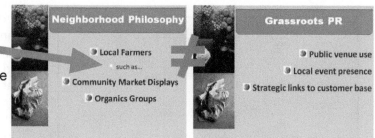

- use the same location/layout for headers, bullets, textboxes, and other text
- do not have images with multiple looks (e.g., some are black and white with a 1950's motif while others are neon colors with various geometric shapes)
- keep your font type and sizes consistent between slides

EEK... VISUAL USE OF BULLET *TYPE* DOES NOT MAKE LOGICAL SENSE

When you first learned to write an outline, your teachers schooled you on "levels." They told you that each level or argument rank should be represented with the same level of Roman Numeral or same type of lettering. In a Word document, you may be familiar with outlining options.

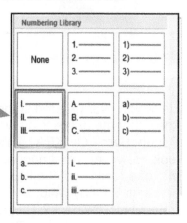

Unfortunately, when you select to bullet a list in PowerPoint, your "outline" is given the same bullets throughout (i.e., A, A, A, A, or II, II, II, II, II). That doesn't make much logical sense. It's up to you to make adjustments to your slides so that the levels of arguments are both clear and consistent throughout your talk.

Be consistent <u>across all slides in your presentation</u>. But DO NOT keep the same bullet type PER LEVEL or just change font size. Here some examples of "Bullet Confusion":

(ALL Apples)

(ALL Dots)

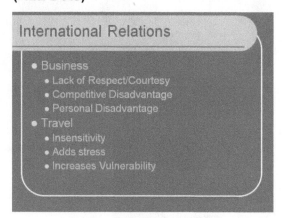

Remember to change the size of bullets *per level*.

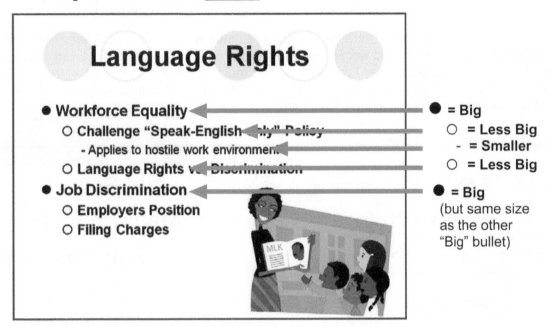

(yeah, yeah… the template has no audience and it is a horrible slide. Good catch! This is just an example of levels.) ☺

As you can see, creating audience-centered templates and keeping the layout of the slide consistent with the verbal outline are the two most basic and crucial elements of slide creation. Sadly, they are often the two most ignored elements of PowerPoint slides. Once you have this big picture mastered, it is time to layer on the other building blocks of your slides in order to finish you slide creation.

TEXTING, TEXTING, TEXTING

Many critics of PowerPoint "how-to" books note the oddity of explaining how to use text on slides *before* discussing visuals when, in fact, PowerPoint is a *visual medium*. Touché! This is a fantastic point – especially when some PowerPoint slides may contain no text at all. The answer to questions of organization is this:

> **Speeches should come before visual aids.** Visual aids… aid. As such, the written work is already done. If you decide, therefore, to use text – you would clarify your ideas by placing the text in your slides *before* placing your visuals. If you choose *not* to use text, it is because you are replacing or *representing* text WITH visuals. An initial discussion of organization, followed by discussions of text and then images keeps the slide logos, purpose, and construction process clear.

If you make a decision to use text on your slides, you must follow two basic rules:
1. **Be Simple**
2. **Be Clear and Legible**

BE SIMPLE

You may vaguely remember (from the constant reminders, thus far) that PowerPoint is a visual medium. If you choose to add words, you must remember that too many of them causes a big disconnect with your audience. You can't ask too much at once of the group in front of you. If you put a book on your slides then you are asking them to read (the slides), listen (to you), look (at the pictures), …. and retain. It's too much.

NOT TOO MUCH TEXT

The 6 X 6 Rule ➡

A basic rule from visual aids created long before PowerPoint is the 6 X 6 rule. This means that there should be:

- no more than 6 words Across a line and
- no more than 6 words that go Down a slide (not counting the header)

For example, this slide has very limited text: *5 words Down and 3 words Across*

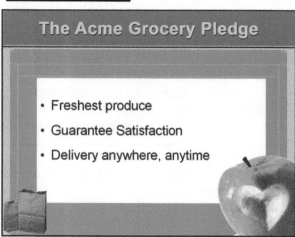

PowerPoint New Math

If you are doing a quick calculation in your head then you have likely realized that 6 X 6 = 36. Ah ha….in PowerPoint we do the "new math." If you were to create a slide with 36 words then you would have a pretty dang overwhelming slide. Too much for your audiences. Instead, practice **no more than 25 words on a slide**. Now that's manageable!

See how editing can help get your audience to quickly grab the information and get right back to you! (Your slides *do not need to be full sentences from your notes*. Edit a bit and keep to key words.) Remember that these aid your talk but the focus should stay on you.

Too Many Words

The Acme Grocery Pledge

- We promise to offer you only the freshest produce available from any grocer
- We unconditionally guarantee your complete and total satisfaction
- We will deliver your groceries to you anywhere, anytime

Ah – Just Right

The Acme Grocery Pledge

- Freshest produce
- Guarantee Satisfaction
- Delivery anywhere, anytime

AVOID TOO MUCH ANIMATION

Just like too many words will make your audiences panic, too much animation might make them run for the hills. Animation is the act of bringing in your text either line-by-line or word by word rather than all at once as you show each slide (not to be confused with transitions, which are how you move between slides). Some animation can be a great way to keep your audience's attention on the exact thing that you are saying – too much can make them, well, giggle.

The easiest way to animate is to:
1. Select the text that you want to animate
2. Choose the "Animations" Tab
3. Select Custom Animation
4. Choose Add Effect (and select Entrance, Exit, or Emphasis, as appropriate)
5. Bring in by levels by selecting the arrow down key and Selecting to "Start On Click" for each Level/ Bullet.

Some options for avoiding distractions are:

Avoid Too Many Types of Animation

Each time you change things up on your audience, they take time to adjust. That's time away from listening to you. Each new animation or switch between types takes adjustment (even just a moment or two). Don't give audiences anything to draw their attention away. Select one or **_maybe_** two ways to bring in text and visual elements. (e.g., a _Blinds_ for bringing in text and a _Dissolve_ for bring in pictures but nothing else).

Do Some Grouping

Consider bringing in more than one line of text at a time or with other elements such as photos or images (i.e., remember to stay in sync with your talk – only bring in _as_ you talk about them).

1. Click on one element, then hit shift, and click on a second (or multiple other) elements while still holding shift

2. Right click while "in" one of the elements to bring in the format window

3. Select "Group"

Now you have "one" element with which to contend!!

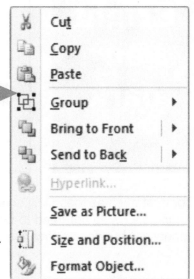

Select Simple Animations
- o some older animations (e.g., Fly, Appear) are overdone and bore
- o some animations take too long (e.g., Diamond, Faded Swivel, Swivel, etc.)
- o some animations are WAY WAY showy, which is another word for annoying (e.g., Pinwheel, Swish, Spinner, etc.)

Some simple animations are Blinds and Dissolve. Try these. They may work for you but if not, think of animation this way... simple. Focus on the talk – not the "show."

WORDART...WHEW!

If showy animation is too much – WordArt is showy text. Like animation, it might be used for a particular purpose (oh, so rarely) but as a rule, it is always best to avoid using something that grabs more attention than your presentation – or something that in many forms has trouble keeping professional appeal. WordArt can be difficult to read your audience will spend too much time processing the "art" rather than listening to you!

BE CLEAR AND BE LEGIBLE

PowerPoint is, yes, a medium that requires simplicity but also one that absolutely necessitates clarity. If your words cannot be read... then why have them?? It is this need for clarity that lends itself to the following:

HAVE STRONG CONTRAST

Contrast is the difference in color between your text and your background color. If they are too close in quality then audiences will spend time trying to decipher them rather than quickly reading and getting back to you. Thus, you must have strong contrast.

For example:

<u>Excellent</u>	<u>Great</u>	<u>Not Bad</u>
Bright on dark	**Dark on Bright**	**Good**
		Good

Contrast such as these will ensure that your audience can quickly read every word. Your combinations do not need to be black and white (in fact, other colors can be more visually appealing) but do not sacrifice clarity for pretty colors! ☺

Things to be careful of

Some backgrounds will make text very difficult to see. Watch out for fades (text will be visible on one part of your slide and not another); low contrast (the text is too closely related in color to the background), or... you will have good contrast but the look will be, er, ugly.

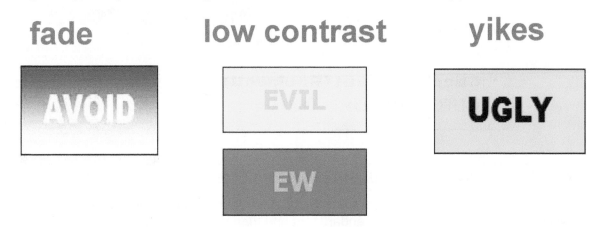

fade   low contrast   yikes

AVOID   EVIL   UGLY

EW

MAKE IT VISIBLE

Sometimes even the best contrast doesn't matter if it is too tiny to see. As you are placing your text (this includes the text on your graphs, charts, or images), think about what can be seen quickly. If you are unsure, print out your slides in full-page version and place them on the floor. Then set a slide at your feet and take **one GIANT step backward**.

Can you still see even the smallest text *easily*?

If not, bump up those sizes. You don't have to go ginormous, just visible.

Stick to:

- Titles (**44** points or bigger)
- Subtitles/ Subpoints (**32** points or bigger)
- Details (**28** points or bigger)
- never below 24 points... even on charts because we *really* need to see those!!

As you adjust your sizes, remember to be consistent across all of your slides. One of the failings of slide creation is when folks adjust their text sizes so that they are more easily seen – but if a phrase doesn't fit... they shrink the size! Everything begins to look random and unorganized.

Consistency is key!

If you need to change your font, (e.g., Arial to Lily to Rockwell to Trajan even if each is in a 32 point size) remember that the size of the words will change. What may be medium size in one font could be **HUGE** or tiny in another font. Double check.

- Check the Font (Arial)
- Check the Font (Lily)
- **Check the Font (Rockwell)**
- CHECK THE FONT (TRAJAN)

all 24 pt font!

Note: YOU MAY GIVE YOUR PRESENTATION ON SOMEONE ELSE'S COMPUTER!

It is important to check that other computers have your fonts. If they aren't standard, PowerPoint will convert them to a standard font and then all your sizing will likely be off – even off your slide! Yet, another good reason to stick to basic fonts.

SERIF AND SANS SERIF – AND OTHER "FONTY" DECISIONS

As you are selecting your fonts, remember that some fonts are meant to be read quickly and others take more time to process. Serif versus Sans Serif font choices will greatly help your clarity. Serifs are those little feet or hanging chads at the end of each stroke. Sans means *without* (in French! Use it often to sound very elegant!) and refers to a font without those little feet. See the examples in the box: (Sans Serif) Arial, Tahoma, Lily, Papyrus / (Serif) Times New Roman, Garamond, Bernard, Rosewood.

Serif font faces take a bit more time to read (like in books!) versus Sans Serif, which can be understood with more of a quick glance (quick! Glance at a street sign... what font is that??? Answer: Arial!! No feet!)

Even if you find fabulous Serif fonts or the audience uses these on a website – choose carefully. Some fonts are easier to read and some are sorta hard to grasp. Choose wisely.

Sans Serif
- The quick brown fox jumps over the lazy dog
- The quick brown fox jumps over the lazy dog
- The quick brown fox jumps over the lazy dog
- The quick brown fox jumps over the lazy dog

- The quick brown fox jumps over the lazy dog
- The quick brown fox jumps over the lazy dog
- **The quick brown fox jumps over the lazy dog**
- THE QUICK BROWN FOX JUMPS OVER THE LAZY DOG

Serif

Consider keeping the visual elements and overall feel of your audience's website or public materials but altering font choices for the majority of your slide text for visual clarity.

Header Talk

Headers are like billboards. They can grab attention or fade into the background – they can clarify or confuse. As noted above, headers that reference "subpoints" or evidence are not appropriate visual cues. Once you have the right text, however, what do you do with it?

DON'T SHOUT! Whether in an email from your friend or a slide presentation, "All caps" will have your audience feel like you are yelling (try not to yell at your audience). Sentence case (capitalizing the first letter of the first word) or capitalizing each word in your header are more inviting formats.

In addition, you may consider asking a question. Questions are fantastic means of engaging your audience – but must be strategically employed. Do these match your presentation? Your argument outline? Be sure to clarify your <u>arguments</u> before making stylistic choices!

NO ORPHANED TEXT

Alas, the last and nearly forgotten element to consider with text is orphans. Orphans are, well, small abandoned children. Orphaned text (a term common in graphic design) refers to *abandoned words*.

These are words that are part of a line of text but, due to the length of the line/ sentence, have dropped on to the next line all by themselves. See that poor "orphans" word on the second line? It is all alone in the world. Sad. Edit that sentence to put it closer to its friend words! ☺

Since folks tend to read down a slide, a word alone will take on an individual meaning and be confusing. In addition, words on a line alone take up space to create an awkward layout for the slide with lots of "dead" space.

BAD

GOOD (see? same idea, rephrased!)

Note: Orphaned text does not refer to lists. We get it. They are meant to be read down and not across. Just be careful what you leave "alone."

PROOFREADING

Now that you have finished creating your text, this last step may be the most important. Proofreading. Yes, you know that you should do it and try to be watchful as you are working through your slides. Yet too often bypassing this final check leads to the dreaded…. typo.

Give your text another go round. Did you say "to" when you meant "too"; did you write "weird" when you meant "wired"; did you leave out the one word that allows everything else make sense, or put an extra space between two words? One last check won't hurt you but not doing it just might.

IMAGES, PICTURES, PHOTOS, AND ART (OH MY!)

We have finally come to the most important part of your slides – the images. Why (if this is so important) is it buried in the middle of this book? Well, the organization HAD to come first – we talked about this! Imagine if you just put a whole bunch of cool pictures up and showed them. People might think, "cool," but they would also think… "and, why am I seeing these?" Your organization gives your images a point and an order. Now you must determine what images to use and how to use them.

FINDING IMAGES

So, we spent some time talking about not stealing (that still applies). You may now be a little baffled about where the heck to get pictures to use for your slides, especially audience-centered images. Do not fret. There is a plethora of places willing to give and to sell you pictures.

As you know, if you are in a classroom, your image use *likely* falls under "Fair Use" protection (at least to a certain extent). Once you leave that setting, however, you may not be able to show your slides to anyone but those who own the images. This sorta defeats the purpose of having some great presentations in your portfolio.

Best to start with legally obtained images ready for use in the long run!

INTERNET

Audience Owned/Linked

If you have permission, then your very best place to find images is from your audience. Go to their website (make sure that they have not purchased images that they do not have the right to give you permission to use… you don't want the photographer hunting you down!), search the internet for images of their events, their logos, and their people. Use those as examples for your talk. This is sure to get the "oh… that's us! That's me!" response to your presentation. Your audience will be totally tuned in. Just remember – permission.

Free Online

If you do not have permission from your audience, then you may wish to turn to the ole "world wide web." This vast space is full of free images put up just for public use. Literally, type the phrase "free images" into any search engine to locate several MILLION websites. For example, http://www.flickr.com/creativecommons/ has millions of photos listed by the type of use allowed (i.e., attribution, noncommercial, no derivative works, or share alike. Descriptions of what each label means are on the Flckr website).

Purchased

Many of the free images that you will find have been used by some several thousand folks (after all, they're free). If you would like to look a bit less like the pack, you may consider purchasing some images. Again, some several thousand other folks have done this before you so even in this mode, you must select your images to do the best that you can to link to the particular audience sitting in front of you.

MICROSOFT POWERPOINT

If you have PowerPoint on your computer, you have access to countless images. The software includes a "Clip Art" insertion (we will talk about the merits and definition of Clip Art later in this section) under the "Insert" Tab that can be searched through for specific images.

CD BOOKS

Any bookseller can offer you an overabundance of books with accompanying CDs that are full of stock images for your use. You can access hard copies of these texts or find online/ downloadable versions of image collections.

For instance, simply type in "stock image cd" when searching on Amazon.com (or other book retailer) and you will find pages of book offerings from general collections to limited compilations of cat images or German houses.

The breadth or depth of your selection is completely up to you. Once you purchase these, they belong to you and you can use them how you see fit.

YOU!!!

Too often, we forget that we are our own best resource. Does anyone not own a camera these days? (If you're wondering, check your cell phone, too! ☺). If you don't take photos, surely your friends have been sending you images of their trips, parties, pets, and activities for quite some time. Start saving them.
Not all of them. ➡

Have a file on your computer where you save the photos that make you laugh or think or could represent something very specific. Save the ones that are beautifully composed. (Be sure to get permission to use these – and, even more so, be professional and ethical in your use.)

You, too, should start to take or save your own images. You can do anything that you want with these: manipulate the color, crop off the sides, distort, change the brightness or contrast, or even combine pictures for a whole new look. This can all be done right in PowerPoint and is totally free.

Note: MAC vs. PC

YOU MAY GIVE YOUR PRESENTATION ON SOMEONE ELSE'S COMPUTER! While you have read this warning for other elements earlier in this book, it is especially crucial to know how to copy, paste, and save images if you are going from MAC to PC.

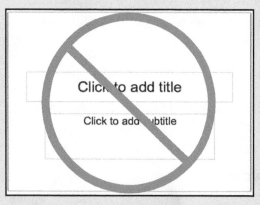

You cannot drag images!! This is a great tool for MAC users but when we switch to a PC, these images come up as empty space holders. Rather than drag, be sure to copy and paste your images so that they may be shown on any type of computer or use the "insert image" function from the images tab.

Some PC to MAC conversions will not work when you have used a Microsoft template that shows pictures. To avoid this, be sure to use a blank slide (no auto-insert boxes) and avoid use of the Master slide. Follow the guidelines from above to create a side and then copy and paste it for use as a template.

HIGH QUALITY

Once you have your images, check to see if they are of high quality. Yes, this is somewhat subjective. That being said, most of us will agree when something is crummy quality – so here are some guidelines to avoid the crum:

Pixels (300x300)

Choose high resolution images. If you select an image online, look at the numbers below it. These will tell you the title, pixels, file size, type of file, and source. Stick to 300 on either side of the "x" to help ensure crisp images.
(Oh… even a large resolution photo not well taken will be fuzzy. Double check how it looks.)

Too Big and Too Small

Yes, size matters – in PowerPoint. If your audience can't see your images because they are too tiny or you have inserted a low pixel image and just stretched it out to make it bigger (and, thus, really fuzzy), well, it matters.

Title

File Size
Type of File

Pixels
Source

…**dog** days of summer – New York Times
1600 x 1200 - 316k - jpg
www.nytimes.com

See what happens when a clear *little* image is stretched big?? He becomes fuzzy! Choose high resolution images and size them to allow them to be clearly seen from the distance of your furthest audience member (typically at least 1/5 of the slide area, which does mean that you must limit the number of pictures per slide).

Big Fuzzy   **Tiny Crisp**

Clip Art is Evil

Many, many, many (ok, most) PowerPoint books will tell you to embrace Clip Art. It is certainly good to feel the love but all images ought to be used thoughtfully. Only a few paragraphs above, you learned of the Clip Art options. If it had no merits, it would not be discussed. So… let's define Clip Art. What PowerPoint has come to offer in this option has changed dramatically since its inception. In early versions, we were treated to classic works such as:

a pointy… "man"??

a "scene" (never sure of what they are, but Microsoft designers seem to love these computer renderings of *thematic events*)

a car (perhaps an early version Ferrari or the new Camero hybrid)

money (or robbing a bank – or, could be someone picking up after their dog with an environmentally friendly bag)

These funky representations of who knows what are traditional Clip Art. They are unclear computer-generated pictures. **Clip Art IS evil.** While your audience is wondering both what and why, you will have lost their attention. Now, we should give credit to Microsoft for updating their image offerings. Today when you click on the same button, you have the option to choose actual pictures but you still have many of these odd creatures. You HAVE options – select what needs no interpretation and grabs!

 VS.  VS.

GRAPHING IT OUT

A good explanatory element can be a well-used graph or chart. You might find that a pie chart helps to show distribution or a line graph clarifies changes over time. The best thing about charts is that they are images that *you create*. As you are determining what chart to put in (and, no, they are not always necessary and can become far more confusing than helpful), be sure to use the best chart in the most illuminating way.

The easiest way to create a chart is to:
1. Select the slide where you want to show your graph/chart
2. Choose the "Insert" Tab and click on "Chart" to bring up the options
   - A blank chart will pop up along with a spreadsheet to complete
3. Fill in data on the spreadsheet... watch the chart change before your very eyes!!

If you have not used a chart before and are not sure what elements to put in which spreadsheet cells, play with it. The image will immediately change to show what you type.

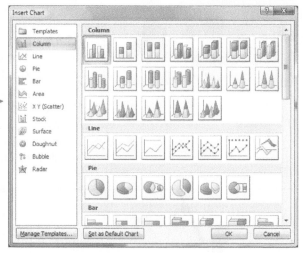

Once you have your information in the chart or graph, you likely will want to alter its appearance for a bit of visual appeal. Right clicking (MAC folks – remember the control key) on the element, such as the font or a particular graph part, will bring up a floating window with format options. Have some fun... but keep your mind on what is helpful rather than what is just fun to create.

EASY!!

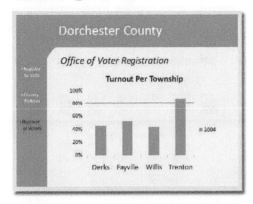

FUN!

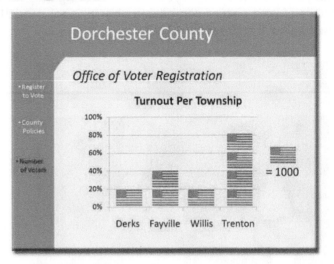

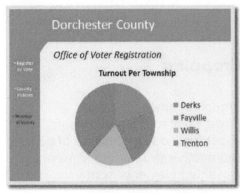

Note: You may be tempted to simply insert another person's chart as an image on your slide. Be sure to follow the guidelines for legally using other's data and images – and, just like with your own graph or chart – alter the text to make it visible to your audience.

(If your copied chart or graph has 13 point font... no one can read it and it will both pull attention away from your talk and diminish the usefulness of the graph itself! Crop out the small text or use a color square to cover the words so that you can re-create them in BIG, VISIBLE sizes!)

ALTERATIONS

Finding pictures is likely not the end of your slide creation story. The pictures that you find may not be in the shape that you want them to be or they could use a bit of enhancement to really grab the audience.

THE "FORMAT" TAB

Only when you select a picture will the "Format" Tab open up in PowerPoint (MAC users will select the image and then open the "Toolbox.") Once it does - it opens up an infinite world of possibilities for manipulating pictures and images. It is likely that you will not use all of those options but there are some basic formatting elements that can help really make images grab your audience.

Recolor

Sometimes what will best make your point is not a picture that you find but one that you create. Altering the smallest details of your picture can have a phenomenal impact! (Just select the "Recolor" option.)

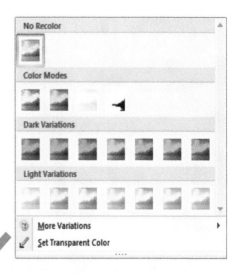

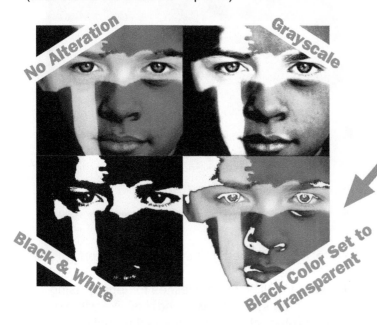

Cropping

Cropping may be the best PowerPoint tool you ever learn about (no kidding)! Instead of going into another program to eliminate unwanted elements from your images, just "Crop" them out.

Now this won't allow you to cut around irregular shapes – it only cuts off the sides but this will make a huge difference in what images you may elect to utilize.

Ordering and Grouping

It is likely that you will have more than one element on your slides. If your pasting does not leave you with the layering effect that you desire, try ordering your elements. Just click on the one that you want your audience to see on top – or put in back – and right click. You will be presented with options to "Bring (the image) to Front" or "Send to Back." MAC users will control click and go to "Arrange."

If you find that you would like to bring in more than one image at the same time, *group* them! Just as was mentioned above in the discussion on animation, one option for bringing items in together is to simply to click on one image, hold the shift key, and click on the next image. While all are still selected, right click to choose Group (MAC users hit click and control.)

Group as many images together as ya like! Now you have <u>one</u> item to move, animate, etc!

To Frame or Not to Frame...

You may elect to "frame" or put a border around your image. This is a very easy step in the "Format" Tab of PowerPoint (select "Picture Border" and choose a line color and weight.) Why?

Well, consider this. If you took a photo, came home, and taped it to the wall, it might be easy for people to see but would it actually draw attention to the image – in a good way? What if instead you popped up to Targét (that's French for the big superstore) and purchased a picture frame for that photo? The entire look of the photo would change and people would be drawn to it in a completely different way. Image frames do the same.

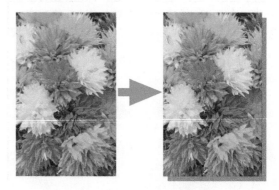

After you have framed your image, you might also want to click on the drop down arrow next to "Picture Effects" and opt for a bit of a shadow (as shown here) for some extra pop!

Framing Irregular Images

The images here are rectangular. If they were irregular then a frame might look, well,... odd. See? Only frame the images that would naturally need a frame!

Note: Keep it simple. <u>The frame should not be what people notice</u> (consider a subtle 1/2 point frame in a grey color – or a color that compliments the photo). However, if you do choose to use a frame, do so consistently with all the photos in your slides. Remember that every change takes time for the audience to adjust.

DRAG FROM THE EDGES

Once you have your image and it's just lovely, it may need some resizing (make it bigger or smaller). One of the classic new users errors is to try to resize an image by first dragging it from the top and then from the bottom. Guess what? Distorted image! Instead, drag from the corners and the sizing will adjust with you!

Dragged from the sides. (Whoops. Fat dog).

PLACEMENT

Finding pictures is likely not the end of your slide creation story. Where do you put them? As noted above, images should take up at least ⅕ of your slide. Think about where on your slide you will put your elements so that the information is clear.

Think of slides like a billboard that drivers will pass quickly on the freeway. If the layout is simple with a fair bit of room on the slide, then those that speed by will be able to grasp your point quickly. Too much on your billboard or oddly placed??? Well, likely drivers will look away.

Too Much

Less Stuff/Better Placement

NO TEXT / LIMITED TEXT

It is very possible that your slides will have no text at all. WHAT??? No text? Don't all slides have text? They do not. As previously noted, PowerPoint is a visual medium and may simply be the means to *literally* illustrating your point. It is important, however, that you do not simply throw pictures up for the sake of having pictures. Using PowerPoint as a solely visual medium still means that you should follow these four guidelines:

1. Follow the verbal outline
2. Be organized
3. Be clear
4. Stay with the theme

The best means of seeing how to make slides that do not use text (or have limited text) is to *see* your options!

Slides with Main Point Titles and Images (no main point text)

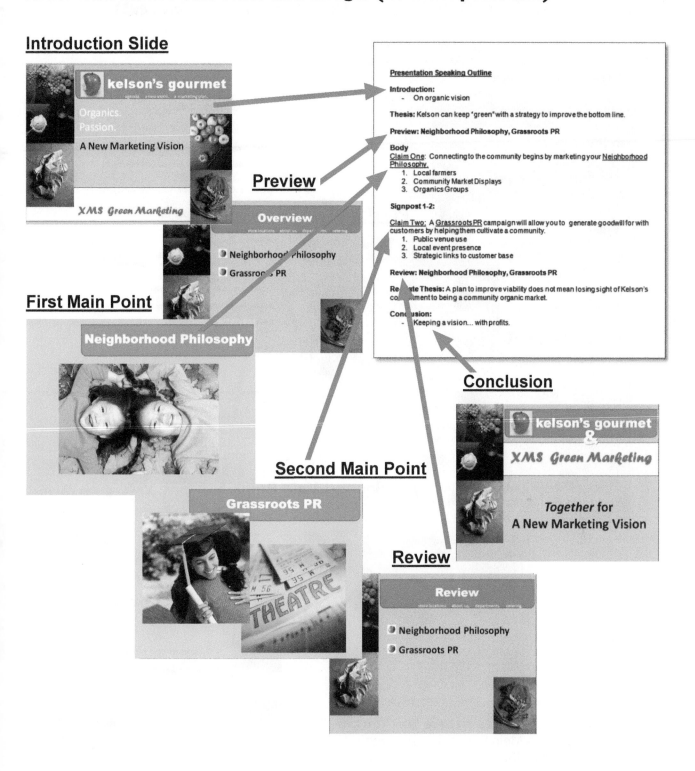

Slides with Images Only for Main Points (no main point text)

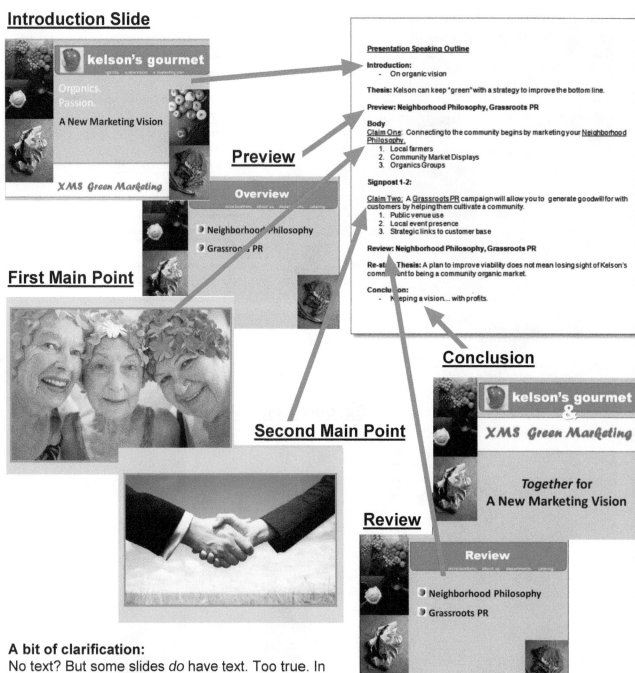

Introduction Slide

Preview

First Main Point

Second Main Point

Conclusion

Review

A bit of clarification:
No text? But some slides *do* have text. Too true. In this example, the Main Points are represented by visuals only while the slides for the Introduction, Preview and Review, and Conclusion utilize text.
The text slides could be eliminated OR be represented by images alone as long as the visual still matches the verbal outline. These slides were left in this version to emphasize that point! ☺

Slides with Images for Main Points and Subpoints / No Text

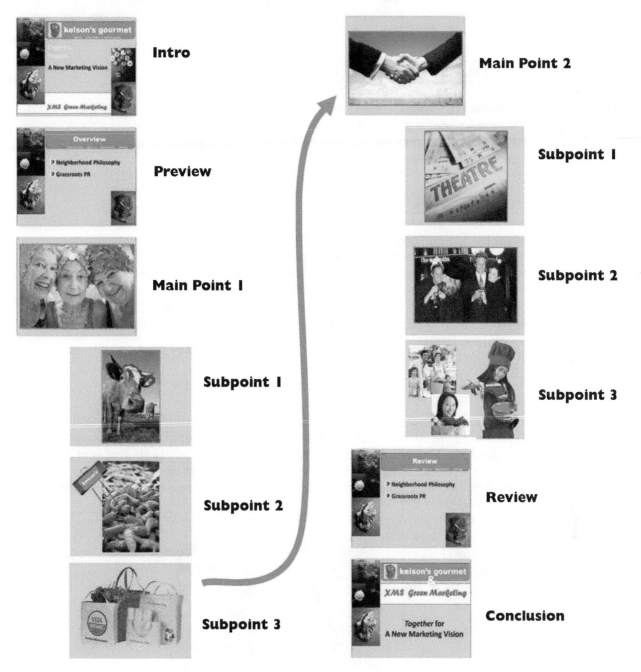

As you can see from the layout represented here, while the slides now contain only visuals (other than the intro and ending slides)… each is clearly linked to the verbal outline and the organization is still evident! Although what you see in these examples are not your only options, they should give you an idea of how to move forward. PowerPoint slides can include moderated text, limited text, or even no text as long as you remember what it is that you are supporting.

And now, you are ready for some bells and whistles!

ADDING

THE BELLS AND THE WHISTLES

This book is about audience. Presenters should be doing everything possible to pull the audience in. Often, in speaking, this means adding a whole lot to capture your listeners. With PowerPoint, however, it typically means adding just a wee bit. Remember to keep the focus on you even as you jazz up your presentation visuals.

ANIMATION AND TRANSITIONS

Animation is different than transitions. Animation refers to the means by which you bring in elements on an individual slide. Transitions are how you move in-between slides. The section on text talked about selecting **simple animations**. This section should only remind you of that edict and note that the concept of simplicity applies to how you move from one slide to the next, too. Slides should generally just appear (no transitions, especially for your first slide, which serves as your backdrop as you begin). Otherwise, keep your choices basic and consistent. Focus on the talk – not the "show."

SOUND

Like animation, in an effort not to distract your audience, sound in PowerPoint must be strategically and sparingly applied. Many of us have sat in a meeting or classroom where the presenter has just learned how to include sound and has done so **for every line of text** or, worse yet, every word. It's like going to the circus!! First there are cameras, then there are drum rolls, then explosions followed by applause – oh my! Audiences would be better captivated if they weren't so busy being appalled. Turn the sound off. If you decide to use it for emphasis, stick to once or maybe twice per show (NOT per slide) is plenty. Better to leave the sound effects to THX.

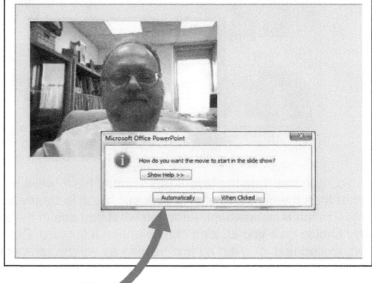

INSERTING VIDEO

Inserting a video is a simple task and somehow always impresses. It is sooooooo easy.

1. Go to the slide where you want the video.
2. Click on the "Insert" Tab
3. Click on Movie
4. Select the Video/ Movie from wherever you have saved it on your computer
5. It will insert and ask....

AUTOPLAY

It is such an amazing idea that as we talk, our slides will simply advance behind us without our help. It's like magic!! Well, magic may have its drawbacks. Consider that when you have your slides or even your bullets animate and transition automatically, you are positive that you will not alter your speech in any way. You will not take an extra breath, elaborate a little less, or… interact with your audience. These things cannot happen if the slides behind you are moving along on their own. Sometimes just doing it ourselves *is* better.

UNEXPECTED EXTRAS

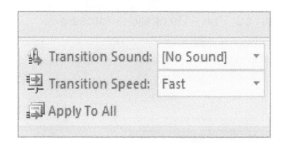

Something else that comes on its own is *embedded* sounds and animation. When you are copying Clip Art from Microsoft or off the internet, be aware that some images will have these extras. You cannot see the auto-animation until the presentation is in the slide show and on the particular slide (i.e., nothing like having your picture start waving to the audience from behind you while you rattle on unaware).

Therefore, it is vital that you run through your presentation with the speakers ON! Who knows what gems you missed during your silent run-through???

TOOOOO MUCH

FILE SIZE

You have learned quite a bit. In fact, too much if you applied every trick. The result would be a monstrous file size. The larger your file size, the slower the show will run during your presentation. If you have seen a presenter hit the space bar to advance slides time and time again and nothing happened, then suddenly the slides shot ahead. The file was too large and the processor was catching up.

Your first option for having a smaller slide show file is to include less on it (less pictures, less animations, *no* movies, etc). Option Two is to compress your pictures.

1. Select a picture
2. Choose the "Format" Tab
3. Click on "Compress Picture"
4. Choose to compress just the one you have selected or all the pictures in your slide show.

(**Note**: Sometimes you will get all the benefits of a smaller file and not visibly see any difference in the picture quality. Other times, the pictures will lose some of their crispness. Save your entire presentation first in one location and then compress a second copy of your original. This will save you if the images end up looking crummy).

LOOK WHAT I CAN DO!

Once you know how to do tons of stuff with PowerPoint, you may be tempted to do it all. This is a classic "adding" error. Like any new toy, we become eager to play with it and show it off. Unfortunately, this creates the disconnect about which Tufte (the critic we talked about in our first few pages) was so eager to tell us. Too much focus on our PowerPoint slides forces a division between speakers and audiences.

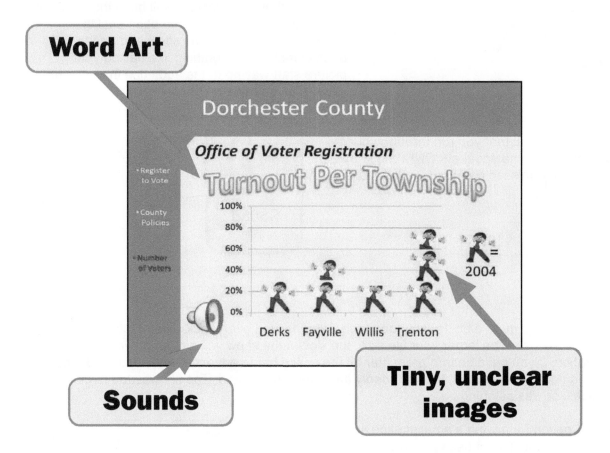

It's an easy fix.

Remember – it's not about you. It's about your audience. Don't show them all your tricks. Show them that you are 100% focused on their needs and that's when they will hang on your every word. Keep it simple.

PRESENTING

DELIVERY

Whoo hoo! Your slides are done! Now what? Well, most PowerPoint books now leave ya hanging. Let's go just a wee bit further (from that communication perspective, again. Don't worry; we won't use the "theory" word). Because your slides are a *part* of your talk, it is crucial that you know how to present them effectively. This includes not allowing them to be the focus of your talk (that's you!) and not allowing them to distract your audience.

INTERACTING WITH YOUR SLIDES

As you begin to practice your presentation (yup – that's a given! Make sure to run through it a few times before actually showing it to an audience), remember that your PowerPoint presentation will give you visual reminders and clarifications of your argument. If you have constructed your slides according to your verbal outline, then you are already in fantastic shape. Now you are in a place to *use* the slides.

Here are some basics:
1. Get the lights right. Be sure to dim or shut off lights prior to starting your talk. PowerPoint presentations are like a romantic date, they need just the right lighting.

2. Know how to get your slide show in presentation mode (er, if you don't know… hit the F5 button to start on slide number 1 or go to the bottom right and click on the screen-looking icon . This will start you on whatever slide you are viewing. MAC users: same button but on the bottom left or ⌘ and return to start from slide 1).

3. Interact with your visuals (talk about what the audience is seeing per slide; look at the slides to make sure that you are not verbally ahead or behind what the audience is following visually. Your audience is looking at those slides… be in sync with them!)

4. Yes, you can touch the screen (point to show your audience what you are talking about – but *avoid* putting your backside to your audience)

5. Don't project on you (get out of the way – let the audience see the slides)

INTERACTING WITH YOUR AUDIENCE

As you know by now, a noteworthy criticism of PowerPoint is that it creates a disconnect between speakers and audiences. It does. In the classroom, you may see students ignore professors while trying to copy every word on every slide without any awareness of the actual lecture. In the boardroom, you regularly can watch eyes glaze over at the beginning of successive slides for sales or department reports.

This is typically because speakers have failed at some of the things that you have already mastered (e.g., being in sync with the verbal, having clear images and organization, etc.). Yet even the most wonderful slide show can disengage an audience. You are a speaker. Be aware of this. Utilize tools that will help keep your audience engaged.

B & W

Learn two amazing buttons that will help focus your audience back on you. The B and W keys allow you to be "in" your presentation but not actually show your slides at that moment.

When your presentation is showing (this won't work in slide sorter or other views), hit B and the screen will go black. To bring it back…. hit the B key again! The same goes for the W key, except that it, obviously, turns the screen white.

Just imagine – you are explaining something and see the audience glaze over. You hit the W key and the room lights up! Now all eyes are back to you. (It's a great trick.) The "B" key works equally as well so that your audience does not see you fumbling to get set up. Go into your room a wee bit early (a good idea anyway to check the set up and become familiar with the setting) and get your slides up and running. Then hit the B key.

When your audience walks in, they see nothing. But when it is time for you to speak, just open your show. No need to show all the slides laid out in slide sorter or giving them a peek at your desktop picture of you at home in your PJs. Instead, just hit the key… and you're on!!

JUMPING SLIDES

Another big criticism of PowerPoint is that it is linear. In other words, some argue that PowerPoint forces the speaker's talk along one path and this path cannot be changed to meet the audience's needs. Pshaw! (That's grandma talk for… nuh uh!!). PowerPoint slides go in the order that you tell them to. Say that you are training a group of sales reps and, as you are about to start, they ask if you can skip to your third point to start. Do not panic! Just do it.

There are many ways to "jump" around in your slide presentation. Most of them involve bringing up a pop up window and clicking on the slide number that you desire. This looks a bit clumsy. Instead, know your slide numbers (bring a print out of all your slides on one page – yes, PowerPoint lets you print like this – or just have a Post-It next to your computer that tells you the slide number where every new discussion point begins. MAC users can cheat a bit. You can use "View Presenter Tools" to see all of your slides while the audience only sees the slide show view). If you know that your third main point begins on slide #24, then once you have finished your introduction simply hit the buttons 2 and 4 and then the Enter key. *Tra la...* you are on slide #24!! (And everyone will just think that you psychically planned your slides just as they would want them).

VIDEO TRANSFERS

Too often folks want to use the captivating elements of a video in their slides but when they go to show it... nothing. There are many reasons that this can happen and a few ways to help to prevent it.

1. Make sure that the computer on which you are showing your slides has the software to show your particular video type (check or ask ahead of time – some video playing software is an easy and free download, but you'll need permission and time).

2. Make sure that the computer can project videos. Sometimes computers and projectors don't like to talk to each other when a video is involved. You may need a tech person with this. However, in an attempt to troubleshoot, try showing only the image from the projector and not viewing it simultaneously on your computer screen. Sometimes this will make them both happy.

3. Save your video and slide show in a FOLDER and then **copy that *folder*** (rather than the slide show alone) onto the computer that you will use. PowerPoint does not actually put videos into presentations. It puts links into your slide show of where to find the video that you wish to play. Thus, when you get to your video and click on it, the computer looks for it saved in a particular location. If that location is on a different computer... it ain't gonna play. If you have inserted it from this folder and PowerPoint is looking in that folder on the new computer – you're in business!

OOOPS'S

The final steps to presenting your PowerPoint show will prevent some embarrassing mistakes. These blunders make the best stories – but not the best impression.

SCREEN SAVERS

Change your screen saver!!!!!!!!!!!!!!! If you are on a slide in your show long enough for the computer to bring up your screen saver, it will. If your screen saver is pictures of you doing the polka at a family wedding or photos of your last beach vacation, then your entire audience may get to know you just a wee bit too well. Make sure that before each presentation you turn off your screen saver (or, better yet, if you know that you will forget, switch it to something professional and appropriate for public viewing).

STAYING IN PLAY

As you enthusiastically run through your slides, you may find that you run right past your last slide. If you are not familiar with this process, try once at home. What will happen is that you will end up in Slide Sorter view. This shows all your slides to your audience and leaves a rather unprofessional final impression. So, try these quick fixes:

Blank Slides

To make sure that this does not happen at the end of your show, have a "Blank" slide at the end of your show. This slide should be the same background color as all of your other slides (plain white would be jarringly different if your slides all have color and attract attention away from your speech). Be sure that this slide is without any pictures or words. It is not a template... just a background color. This extra slide will ensure that if you do jump ahead, you can keep the audience focused on you.

Hit the Slide Show Button – Again

If you are in the middle of your speech and for some reason pop out into the Slide Sorter or individual slide view – GO BACK!

So many speakers just leave the slides in this awkward viewing format. Don't freak, don't make a big deal about, no need to even comment on it. Just walk over and put the show back in slide show view and go to the appropriate slide. Be calm. ☺

"TALKING" POWERPOINT

Just as much as creating a PowerPoint presentation can enhance or detract from your credibility, so can how you "talk" about PowerPoint. If you inaccurately refer to your presentation then you let your audience know that you have not mastered your work in this medium. To help guide you in your talk, Microsoft (the noble providers of PowerPoint) has provided us with the following simple reminders
(adapted from: http://www.microsoft.com/about/legal/trademarks/ usage/powerpoint.mspx):

"PowerPoint is a trademark that identifies a brand of presentation software from Microsoft." In other words, there are certain legal (but also _accurate_) ways to refer to your presentations!

Incorrect:
- "Send me your powerpoints."
- PowerPoints or Power Points (plural)
- PPT
- PPTs
- Powerpoint

Correct:
- "Send me your PowerPoint slides."
- PowerPoint (singular… this is a proper name and should not be pluralized)

Talk like this will always make you the most erudite individual in the room – and you'll sound smart, too! ☺

A FINAL WORD

IT'S ABOUT COMMUNICATION

We have reached the end of our journey and, hopefully, PowerPoint now serves a new purpose for you. PowerPoint ought not to fall into the failings of poor visual quality, disconnected

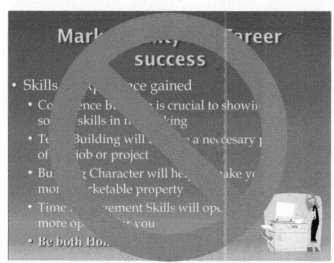

audiences, or limited content – not now that we are doing our part in the process of communication.

No longer should we be subjected to or ever create slides like these! Instead, by approaching PowerPoint through a new lens, we are able to become more effective and perhaps even help others along the way.

Now you know that PowerPoint is about the audience, to the audience, and *for* the audience. It is about bringing our verbal arguments to a visual place; it is not about us.

Remember what you have learned in these pages. You have:
- a simple means of connecting you to your audience
- step by step instructions for creating <u>audience-centered</u> templates
- tools for altering images *without* the need of other software
- a clear understanding of how slides work *with* your speech
- comfortable delivery techniques that will differentiate you from other presenters
- (of course) a few tricks.

As you continue to craft messages through this medium – have some fun! Play with all that this tool has to offer. As with anything, practice makes better. Your visual messages will improve and the ease with which you create them *will* increase.

Part D: 2014-2015 Forms

*The following forms are provided for your use in your SPK 230 course. You should review them ahead of time so that you are familiar with the areas of evaluation for your presentations and to be sure that you have ALL necessary forms! (**Do not buy a used packet that is missing forms or does not have the updates from this semester**!!)*

On the day of your speech, you will need to remove the appropriate evaluation and give it to your professor (he or she will not have copies of this form) along with any other materials required in your SPK 230 section.

Speech Outline Worksheet #1

[This worksheet includes all basic speaking elements. Your speech will include the number of main points necessary to support your thesis, which could be more or less, and abide by all instructor/ section criteria. This worksheet will help you get started in the process including being typed when handed in.)

Topic: Student Name: _____
General Purpose:
Specific Purpose:
Type of Speech Structure Used:

Introduction:
1. Attention-Getter:

2. Credibility:

3. WIFM/Relevance:

Thesis:

Preview:

Body of the Speech

- Claim One/ Argument: _____
- Internal preview:

(sub-points/ support with citations for all evidence offered)
    1.

    2.

    3.
*(add more sub-points as necessary to substantiate your argument)

Transition 1-2:

- Claim Two/ Argument: _____
- Internal preview:

(sub-points/ support with citations for all evidence offered)
    1.

2.

3.
(add more sub-points as necessary to substantiate your argument)

Transition 2-3:

- Claim Three / Argument: _____
- Internal preview:

(sub-points/ support with citations for all evidence offered)
1.

2.

3.
(add more sub-points as necessary to substantiate your argument)

(add more main points as necessary)

Review:

Rephrased Thesis:

Conclusion (link to opening):

Speech Outline Worksheet #2

[This worksheet includes all basic speaking elements. Your speech will include the number of main points necessary to support your thesis, which could be more or less, and abide by all instructor/ section criteria. This worksheet will help you get started in the process including being typed when handed in.)

Topic: Student Name: _____
General Purpose:
Specific Purpose:
Type of Speech Structure Used:

Introduction:
1. Attention-Getter:

2. Credibility:

3. WIFM/Relevance:

Thesis:

Preview:

Body of the Speech

- Claim One/ Argument: _____
- Internal preview:

(sub-points/ support with citations for all evidence offered)
    1.

    2.

    3.
*(add more sub-points as necessary to substantiate your argument)

Transition 1-2:

- Claim Two/ Argument: _____
- Internal preview:

(sub-points/ support with citations for all evidence offered)
    1.

    2.

    3.

(add more sub-points as necessary to substantiate your argument)

Transition 2-3:

- Claim Three / Argument: _____
- Internal preview:

(sub-points/ support with citations for all evidence offered)
    1.

    2.

    3.
(add more sub-points as necessary to substantiate your argument)

(add more main points as necessary)

Review:

Rephrased Thesis:

Conclusion (link to opening):

2014-2015 Speech Self-Evaluation

Reflecting on your presentation(s) will help you to improve on needed areas in your speech as well as consistently continue to use the presentation elements that serve you well with your audience.

Please conduct a self-evaluation of your presentation (due on the date indicated by your individual section instructor). Type up, using the appropriate header and varying in length between 1-2 single spaced pages (page length may vary for individual instructors), the answers to the following questions.

Preparation
1. What steps did you take to prepare this presentation that worked to help improve the content and delivery of your material?
2. What steps did you take or steps did you fail to take in preparing your talk that did not help you and you would like to alter for future presentations?

Presentation
3. Were there any elements of your presentation delivery that you, in reflecting on your own speech or watching the video, were distracting to your audience?
4. What elements of your delivery do you believe helped to enhance your connection to the audience and why?
5. How did you feel after you watched your video of the presentation? Did it go as well or look as you planned or expected? Why or why not?

Big Picture Strategies
6. What two specific goals do you have for yourself as a speaker in a professional speaking environment and how can you go about achieving them?
7. What, if anything, could your instructor have done to make this project a better or more effective experience for you (or your group)?

SPK 230 2014-2015 Résumé Evaluation Form

Student Name: _____ Section:_____ Grade: _____

	Excellent Elements (Can help get you the interview)	Average Elements (May prevent get you from getting the interview)	Problematic Elements (Will most likely prevent you from getting the interview)
Format, Layout, & Style	__ Individualized design. __ Organized layout, spacing, & alignment that enhances readability. __ Appropriate structure (functional/chronological) __ Limited, consistent use of font styles (italic, bold, underline) that improve readability __ Font size varies appropriately b/w headings and content	__ Minimal problems with layout, spacing, & alignment but readability is not inhibited __ Not clear or poor choice of structure __ Some overuse or inconsistent font use. __ Font size variation inhibits readability	__ Use of pre-existing template __ Problems in format, layout, spacing, or alignment that inhibit readability __ Significant structure issues __ Overuse and/or inconsistent font use that hurts readability
Industry Link	__ Section titles and details/content all show a specific link to the desired industry	__ Section titles and details/content show some link to the desired industry	__ Section titles and details/content are not clearly linked to the desired industry
Appropriate Language	__ Use of action terms that demonstrate tone __ Terms that link to the job description __ No negative details __ No irrelevant details __ Accurate grammar, vocabulary (e.g., word forms, word choice) __ Verb/tense matches	__ More action terms needed __ Not clear job description terms __ A few negative or irrelevant details __ Some minor grammar, vocabulary, and/or verb or tense inaccuracies	__ Need clear action terms __ Terms do not link to the job description __ Negative detail use __ Significant irrelevant details __ Significant grammar or language issues __ Verb or tense inaccuracies
Fitting Details	__ Clear, well-developed descriptions that give a strong sense of the experience __ Includes all required details for education, contact, experience, etc.	__ Need some content/ description development __ Missing some required details for education, contact, experience, etc.	__ Need significant content/ description development __ Missing significant required details
Profession-alism	__ Clean print out & paper __ No errors or typos __ Résumé paper (as required)	← notes (optional) →	__ Poor print out or paper __ Errors or typos __ No résumé paper (as required)
Specific Assignment Criteria	__ Meets specific instructor requirements (e.g., page number, term use, etc.		__ Does not meet specific instructor requirements (e.g., page number, term use, etc.)

SPK 230 2014-2015 Peer Evaluation Forms

Name of speaker:

Type of speech:

1. Content Strength:
(e.g., transitions, source citations & ethos, thesis clarity, organization, argument strength, etc.)

2. Content to Improve:

3. Delivery Strengths and Areas to Improve:
(e.g., eye contact, pronunciation, articulation, speaking rate, gestures, limited notes, expressions, enthusiasm, etc.)

Name of speaker:

Type of speech:

1. Content Strength:
(e.g., transitions, source citations & ethos, thesis clarity, organization, argument strength, etc.)

2. Content to Improve:

3. Delivery Strengths and Areas to Improve:
(e.g., eye contact, pronunciation, articulation, speaking rate, gestures, limited notes, expressions, enthusiasm, etc.)

Name of speaker:

Type of speech:

1. Content Strength:
(e.g., transitions, source citations & ethos, thesis clarity, organization, argument strength, etc.)

2. Content to Improve:

3. Delivery Strengths and Areas to Improve:
(e.g., eye contact, pronunciation, articulation, speaking rate, gestures, limited notes, expressions, enthusiasm, etc.)

Name of speaker:

Type of speech:

1. Content Strength:
(e.g., transitions, source citations & ethos, thesis clarity, organization, argument strength, etc.)

2. Content to Improve:

3. Delivery Strengths and Areas to Improve:
(e.g., eye contact, pronunciation, articulation, speaking rate, gestures, limited notes, expressions, enthusiasm, etc.)

SPK 230 2014-2015 Peer Evaluation Forms

Name of speaker:

Type of speech:

1. Content Strength:
(e.g., transitions, source citations & ethos, thesis clarity, organization, argument strength, etc.)

2. Content to Improve:

3. Delivery Strengths and Areas to Improve:
(e.g., eye contact, pronunciation, articulation, speaking rate, gestures, limited notes, expressions, enthusiasm, etc.)

Name of speaker:

Type of speech:

1. Content Strength:
(e.g., transitions, source citations & ethos, thesis clarity, organization, argument strength, etc.)

2. Content to Improve:

3. Delivery Strengths and Areas to Improve:
(e.g., eye contact, pronunciation, articulation, speaking rate, gestures, limited notes, expressions, enthusiasm, etc.)

Name of speaker:

Type of speech:

1. Content Strength:
(e.g., transitions, source citations & ethos, thesis clarity, organization, argument strength, etc.)

2. Content to Improve:

3. Delivery Strengths and Areas to Improve:
(e.g., eye contact, pronunciation, articulation, speaking rate, gestures, limited notes, expressions, enthusiasm, etc.)

Name of speaker:

Type of speech:

1. Content Strength:
(e.g., transitions, source citations & ethos, thesis clarity, organization, argument strength, etc.)

2. Content to Improve:

3. Delivery Strengths and Areas to Improve:
(e.g., eye contact, pronunciation, articulation, speaking rate, gestures, limited notes, expressions, enthusiasm, etc.)

SPK 230 2014-2015 Peer Evaluation Forms

Name of speaker:

Type of speech:

1. Content Strength:
(e.g., transitions, source citations & ethos, thesis clarity, organization, argument strength, etc.)

2. Content to Improve:

3. Delivery Strengths and Areas to Improve:
(e.g., eye contact, pronunciation, articulation, speaking rate, gestures, limited notes, expressions, enthusiasm, etc.)

Name of speaker:

Type of speech:

1. Content Strength:
(e.g., transitions, source citations & ethos, thesis clarity, organization, argument strength, etc.)

2. Content to Improve:

3. Delivery Strengths and Areas to Improve:
(e.g., eye contact, pronunciation, articulation, speaking rate, gestures, limited notes, expressions, enthusiasm, etc.)

Name of speaker:

Type of speech:

1. Content Strength:
(e.g., transitions, source citations & ethos, thesis clarity, organization, argument strength, etc.)

2. Content to Improve:

3. Delivery Strengths and Areas to Improve:
(e.g., eye contact, pronunciation, articulation, speaking rate, gestures, limited notes, expressions, enthusiasm, etc.)

Name of speaker:

Type of speech:

1. Content Strength:
(e.g., transitions, source citations & ethos, thesis clarity, organization, argument strength, etc.)

2. Content to Improve:

3. Delivery Strengths and Areas to Improve:
(e.g., eye contact, pronunciation, articulation, speaking rate, gestures, limited notes, expressions, enthusiasm, etc.)

SPK 230 2014-2015 Peer Evaluation Forms

Name of speaker:

Type of speech:

1. Content Strength:
(e.g., transitions, source citations & ethos, thesis clarity, organization, argument strength, etc.)

2. Content to Improve:

3. Delivery Strengths and Areas to Improve:
(e.g., eye contact, pronunciation, articulation, speaking rate, gestures, limited notes, expressions, enthusiasm, etc.)

Name of speaker:

Type of speech:

1. Content Strength:
(e.g., transitions, source citations & ethos, thesis clarity, organization, argument strength, etc.)

2. Content to Improve:

3. Delivery Strengths and Areas to Improve:
(e.g., eye contact, pronunciation, articulation, speaking rate, gestures, limited notes, expressions, enthusiasm, etc.)

Name of speaker:

Type of speech:

1. Content Strength:
(e.g., transitions, source citations & ethos, thesis clarity, organization, argument strength, etc.)

2. Content to Improve:

3. Delivery Strengths and Areas to Improve:
(e.g., eye contact, pronunciation, articulation, speaking rate, gestures, limited notes, expressions, enthusiasm, etc.)

Name of speaker:

Type of speech:

1. Content Strength:
(e.g., transitions, source citations & ethos, thesis clarity, organization, argument strength, etc.)

2. Content to Improve:

3. Delivery Strengths and Areas to Improve:
(e.g., eye contact, pronunciation, articulation, speaking rate, gestures, limited notes, expressions, enthusiasm, etc.)

SPK 230 2014-2015 Peer Evaluation Forms

Name of speaker:

Type of speech:

1. Content Strength:
(e.g., transitions, source citations & ethos, thesis clarity, organization, argument strength, etc.)

2. Content to Improve:

3. Delivery Strengths and Areas to Improve:
(e.g., eye contact, pronunciation, articulation, speaking rate, gestures, limited notes, expressions, enthusiasm, etc.)

Name of speaker:

Type of speech:

1. Content Strength:
(e.g., transitions, source citations & ethos, thesis clarity, organization, argument strength, etc.)

2. Content to Improve:

3. Delivery Strengths and Areas to Improve:
(e.g., eye contact, pronunciation, articulation, speaking rate, gestures, limited notes, expressions, enthusiasm, etc.)

Name of speaker:

Type of speech:

1. Content Strength:
(e.g., transitions, source citations & ethos, thesis clarity, organization, argument strength, etc.)

2. Content to Improve:

3. Delivery Strengths and Areas to Improve:
(e.g., eye contact, pronunciation, articulation, speaking rate, gestures, limited notes, expressions, enthusiasm, etc.)

Name of speaker:

Type of speech:

1. Content Strength:
(e.g., transitions, source citations & ethos, thesis clarity, organization, argument strength, etc.)

2. Content to Improve:

3. Delivery Strengths and Areas to Improve:
(e.g., eye contact, pronunciation, articulation, speaking rate, gestures, limited notes, expressions, enthusiasm, etc.)

SPK 230 2014-2015 Peer Evaluation Forms

Name of speaker:

Type of speech:

1. Content Strength:
(e.g., transitions, source citations & ethos, thesis clarity, organization, argument strength, etc.)

2. Content to Improve:

3. Delivery Strengths and Areas to Improve:
(e.g., eye contact, pronunciation, articulation, speaking rate, gestures, limited notes, expressions, enthusiasm, etc.)

Name of speaker:

Type of speech:

1. Content Strength:
(e.g., transitions, source citations & ethos, thesis clarity, organization, argument strength, etc.)

2. Content to Improve:

3. Delivery Strengths and Areas to Improve:
(e.g., eye contact, pronunciation, articulation, speaking rate, gestures, limited notes, expressions, enthusiasm, etc.)

Name of speaker:

Type of speech:

1. Content Strength:
(e.g., transitions, source citations & ethos, thesis clarity, organization, argument strength, etc.)

2. Content to Improve:

3. Delivery Strengths and Areas to Improve:
(e.g., eye contact, pronunciation, articulation, speaking rate, gestures, limited notes, expressions, enthusiasm, etc.)

Name of speaker:

Type of speech:

1. Content Strength:
(e.g., transitions, source citations & ethos, thesis clarity, organization, argument strength, etc.)

2. Content to Improve:

3. Delivery Strengths and Areas to Improve:
(e.g., eye contact, pronunciation, articulation, speaking rate, gestures, limited notes, expressions, enthusiasm, etc.)

SPK 230 2014-2015 Peer Evaluation Forms

Name of speaker:

Type of speech:

1. Content Strength:
(e.g., transitions, source citations & ethos, thesis clarity, organization, argument strength, etc.)

2. Content to Improve:

3. Delivery Strengths and Areas to Improve:
(e.g., eye contact, pronunciation, articulation, speaking rate, gestures, limited notes, expressions, enthusiasm, etc.)

Name of speaker:

Type of speech:

1. Content Strength:
(e.g., transitions, source citations & ethos, thesis clarity, organization, argument strength, etc.)

2. Content to Improve:

3. Delivery Strengths and Areas to Improve:
(e.g., eye contact, pronunciation, articulation, speaking rate, gestures, limited notes, expressions, enthusiasm, etc.)

Name of speaker:

Type of speech:

1. Content Strength:
(e.g., transitions, source citations & ethos, thesis clarity, organization, argument strength, etc.)

2. Content to Improve:

3. Delivery Strengths and Areas to Improve:
(e.g., eye contact, pronunciation, articulation, speaking rate, gestures, limited notes, expressions, enthusiasm, etc.)

Name of speaker:

Type of speech:

1. Content Strength:
(e.g., transitions, source citations & ethos, thesis clarity, organization, argument strength, etc.)

2. Content to Improve:

3. Delivery Strengths and Areas to Improve:
(e.g., eye contact, pronunciation, articulation, speaking rate, gestures, limited notes, expressions, enthusiasm, etc.)

2014-2015 SPK 230 Speech Evaluation Form

Name(s): _____ Section:____ Speech length: _____ Grade: ___ / ___

Speech Purpose/Type: _____ Preparation materials (optional): _____/_____

	Excellent	Average	Needs Improvement
		Organization	
Basic Intro. Elements	❑ **Opening/ attention-getter** effectively draws in the the audience to the topic in a compelling, unique, and inviting manner.	❑ **Opening/ attention-getter** is clearly identifiable, but does not draw in the audience in a compelling, unique, or inviting manner; distracts the audience or needs some development.	❑ **Opening/ attention-getter** is not present, is unrelated to the thesis argument, or significantly distracts the audience.
	❑ Speaker effectively establishes his or her **credibility** to speak on the topic.	❑ Speaker cites credentials or research, but not effectively establish **credibility** to present the topic.	❑ There is no **credibility** statement.
	❑ The speaker effectively establishes why the message is relevant to the audience/ **WIIFM**.	❑ The speaker does not clearly establish the **WIIFM** message to the audience.	❑ There is no **WIIFM** statement or it detracts from the message.
	❑ The **thesis** statement articulates an argument that clearly reflects the rhetorical purpose of the speech.	❑ The **thesis** statement is ambiguous or unfocused, or does not clearly reflect the purpose of the speech.	❑ There is no clear **thesis** statement.
	❑ **Preview** is a very brief statement that identifies the subject of each main point, in the order in which they will be presented in the speech.	❑ **Preview** is hard for the audience to identify, is not presented in the same order as the main points, or is lengthy.	❑ There is no **preview** or the preview is presented in a broad, generalized statement.
Well Organized Speech Body	❑ **Main points** effectively use an easily-identifiable organizational pattern (chronological, motivated sequence, etc.) appropriate for the rhetorical purpose; Internal details are clearly organized.	❑ **Main points** are clearly identifiable, but are not arranged according to a specific pattern; Internal information is not organized in an obvious structure.	❑ **Main points** are not identifiable, blend together, and/or are not arranged according to a specific pattern; Internal details show no organizational order.
	❑ (optional) Clearly and effectively asks the audience to **take a specific action**.	❑ (optional) **Action** request is ambiguous, or not audience specific.	❑ (optional) The **action** request is missing or not feasible.
	❑ **Transitions** make clear, brief links between main points using claim keywords; **internal transitions** are used within main points to organize and link sub-points.	❑ **Transitions** are identifiable but lengthy, ambiguous, or use terminology not linked to claims; **internal transitions** are difficult to identify.	❑ **Transitions** are not present or difficult to identify; **internal transitions** are missing.
Basic Conc. Elements	❑ Briefly **summarizes** main points in order and using claim language.	❑ **Summarizes** each main point, but the review is hard to identify, not linked to claim language, or is not presented in the same order as the main points.	❑ There is no **summary**, or summary is presented in a broad, generalized statement.
	❑ **Closing** effectively wraps up the speech by linking to the opening and leaving a lasting impression.	❑ **Clincher** is identifiable, but does not leave a lasting impression or link to the opening.	❑ There is no clear **clincher**, and/or the speech ends abruptly.
		Content	
Thorough Development of Content	❑ Effectively focuses the topic and content of the speech toward a **specific audience**.	❑ Either the topic or the content does not take the **audience** into consideration.	❑ The **audience** is not taken into consideration.
	❑ **Arguments/ claims are well developed.** Main points are framed by strong claims/ arguments that support the thesis, sub-points effectively support the arguments contained in the main points.	❑ **Arguments/claims are ambiguous**, unfocused, or do not support the thesis; sub-points support of the claims needs clarity.	❑ **Arguments/ claims are missing or ineffective**; sub-points or do not support claims.
	❑ Uses significant **supporting arguments & ideas** (e.g., analogies, narratives, statistics, testimony, etc.) of the highest quality that build audience interest and enhance understanding; establishes strong pathos.	❑ Uses some **supporting arguments & ideas** of good quality that build audience some interest or help a bit with understanding; establishes some pathos.	❑ Uses few or no **supporting arguments & ideas**; ideas are of poor quality, do not build audience interest/ knowledge; limited or not pathos.
	❑ Ethically uses **more than the required #** of **external sources & evidence** derived from current, relevant high-quality research. ❑ Verbally cites and qualifies all sources.	❑ Ethically uses **at least the required #** of **external evidence & sources** derived from good quality research. ❑ Verbally cites all sources.	❑ Uses **less than the required #** of **sources**; poor source ethos. ❑ Does not verbally cite all sources.

Student Name(s): _____   Section:_____

	Excellent	Average	Needs Improvement
Thorough Development of Content (cont....)	❏ Appropriate **word choice** that is vivid and effectively expresses the speaker ideas. ❏ Language is linked to both the speaker and audience and builds credibility.	❏ **Word choice** is appropriate for the speaker and the audience; but language could be more vivid or effectively express ideas.	❏ **Word choice** is not appropriate and/or language use is not vivid or effective.
	❏ **Audio/visual aids** greatly improve listener comprehension and retention of the message. ❏ **Audio/visual aids** adhere to all communication design criteria. **(PPT aids evaluated on separate form)**	❏ **Audio/visual aids** improve listener memory or comprehension, but could be improved or violate some design criteria. **(PPT aids evaluated on separate form)**	❏ **Audio/visual aids** distract or violate significant design criteria. **(PPT evaluated on separate form)**
	❏ Stays within required **time** limits.		❏ Does not stay within required **time** limits.
	Delivery		
Effective Style	❏ Makes effective and appropriate **appearance** choices including clothing (business-casual) and grooming.	❏ **Appearance**, clothing, or grooming are not quite appropriate.	❏ Clearly inappropriate **appearance** choices for the assignment.
	❏ **Facial expressions** link to the message and reflect engagement with the audience.	❏ **Facial expressions** are appropriate but could better connect to the message or audience.	❏ **Facial expressions** are ineffective or inappropriate.
	❏ Maintains direct **eye contact** in a way that engages and interacts with the audience ❏ Holds contact through audience feedback.	❏ Makes some **eye contact**, but is not fully engaged or only directs eye contact to part of the audience.	❏ Makes little to no **eye contact**.
	❏ Uses **limited notes/outline** in an effective way that enhances verbal and nonverbal engagement.	❏ Uses **limited outline/notes** but remains tied to notes in a way that interferes with other delivery elements.	❏ **Outline/notes** inhibit other delivery elements.
	❏ Physical **gestures** emphasize important points and/or transitions, engage listeners, reflect a speaker who is comfortable and at ease. ❏ Select **movement** helps to engage the audience.	❏ Speaker makes an effort with **gestures** and/or physical **movement**, but they do not serve to engage listeners or reinforce the message.	❏ **Gestures** and/or **movements** are overly distracting or ineffective.
	❏ **Volume** is appropriate to the message, audience, room, and mood.	❏ **Volume** is too strong or too soft, or is not appropriate to rhetorical situation.	❏ Speaker **volume** overwhelms the audience or the message cannot be heard.
	❏ **Speaking rate/pace** enhances the message and engages the audience.	❏ **Speaking pace** is overall or in parts either a bit too fast or slow.	❏ **Pace** is either so speedy or slow that it significantly inhibits the message.
	❏ Overall **articulation** and **enunciation** strengthen the clarity of the message. ❏ All terms and names are correctly **pronounced**.	❏ Issues with **articulation** makes it hard to distinguish words and/ or limited **enunciation** inhibits message clarity in parts of the speech. ❏ Some terms incorrectly **pronounced**.	❏ Overall poor **articulation** and/or **enunciation** throughout the speech. ❏ Significant **pronunciation** issues.
	❏ **Vocal tone** adds warmth and interest, helps entice the audience.	❏ Speaker has some **tonal variety**, but could use improvement.	❏ **Monotone** delivery style or **distracting vocal elements**.
	❏ Speaker maintains a **conversational delivery** throughout the speech.	❏ Speaker achieves **conversational delivery** at times, but needs consistency.	❏ Delivery is not **conversational**.
	❏ Speaker is **enthusiastic**. ❏ Speaker is **confident**.	❏ Displays some **enthusiasm**. ❏ Exhibits some **confidence**.	❏ Speaker is **not enthusiastic**. ❏ Speaker is **not confident**.
Group (optional)	❏ Group delivery is consistent, well-rehearsed, and flows as a single speech.	❏ Group delivery is somewhat inconsistent, lacks rehearsal, and/or does not flow as a speech.	❏ Group delivery is inconsistent, unrehearsed, and/or does not flow as a single speech.
Comments (optional)			

2014-2015 SPK 230 Speech Evaluation Form

Name(s): _____ Section:____ Speech length: _____ Grade: ____ / ____

Speech Purpose/Type: _____ Preparation materials (optional): _____/_____

	Excellent	Average	Needs Improvement
Organization			
Basic Intro. Elements	☐ **Opening/ attention-getter** effectively draws in the the audience to the topic in a compelling, unique, and inviting manner.	☐ **Opening/ attention-getter** is clearly identifiable, but does not draw in the audience in a compelling, unique, or inviting manner; distracts the audience or needs some development.	☐ **Opening/ attention-getter** is not present, is unrelated to the thesis argument, or significantly distracts the audience.
	☐ Speaker effectively establishes his or her **credibility** to speak on the topic.	☐ Speaker cites credentials or research, but not effectively establish **credibility** to present the topic.	☐ There is no **credibility** statement.
	☐ The speaker effectively establishes why the message is relevant to the audience/ **WIIFM.**	☐ The speaker does not clearly establish the **WIIFM** message to the audience.	☐ There is no **WIIFM** statement or it detracts from the message.
	☐ The **thesis** statement articulates an argument that clearly reflects the rhetorical purpose of the speech.	☐ The **thesis** statement is ambiguous or unfocused, or does not clearly reflect the purpose of the speech.	☐ There is no clear **thesis** statement.
	☐ **Preview** is a very brief statement that identifies the subject of each main point, in the order in which they will be presented in the speech.	☐ **Preview** is hard for the audience to identify, is not presented in the same order as the main points, or is lengthy.	☐ There is no **preview** or the preview is presented in a broad, generalized statement.
Well Organized Speech Body	☐ **Main points** effectively use an easily-identifiable organizational pattern (chronological, motivated sequence, etc.) appropriate for the rhetorical purpose; Internal details are clearly organized.	☐ **Main points** are clearly identifiable, but are not arranged according to a specific pattern; Internal information is not organized in an obvious structure.	☐ **Main points** are not identifiable, blend together, and/or are not arranged according to a specific pattern; Internal details show no organizational order.
	☐ (optional) Clearly and effectively asks the audience to **take a specific action**.	☐ (optional) **Action** request is ambiguous, or not audience specific.	☐ (optional) The **action** request is missing or not feasible.
	☐ **Transitions** make clear, brief links between main points using claim keywords; **internal transitions** are used within main points to organize and link sub-points.	☐ **Transitions** are identifiable but lengthy, ambiguous, or use terminology not linked to claims; **internal transitions** are difficult to identify.	☐ **Transitions** are not present or difficult to identify; **internal transitions** are missing.
Basic Conc. Elements	☐ Briefly **summarizes** main points in order and using claim language.	☐ **Summarizes** each main point, but the review is hard to identify, not linked to claim language, or is not presented in the same order as the main points.	☐ There is no **summary**, or summary is presented in a broad, generalized statement.
	☐ **Closing** effectively wraps up the speech by linking to the opening and leaving a lasting impression.	☐ **Clincher** is identifiable, but does not leave a lasting impression or link to the opening.	☐ There is no clear **clincher**, and/or the speech ends abruptly.
Content			
Thorough Development of Content	☐ Effectively focuses the topic and content of the speech toward a **specific audience**.	☐ Either the topic or the content does not take the **audience** into consideration.	☐ The **audience** is not taken into consideration.
	☐ **Arguments/ claims are well developed.** Main points are framed by strong claims/ arguments that support the thesis, sub-points effectively support the arguments contained in the main points.	☐ **Arguments/claims are ambiguous,** unfocused, or do not support the thesis; sub-points support of the claims needs clarity.	☐ **Arguments/ claims are missing or ineffective**; sub-points or do not support claims.
	☐ Uses significant **supporting arguments & ideas** (e.g., analogies, narratives, statistics, testimony, etc.) of the highest quality that build audience interest and enhance understanding; establishes strong pathos.	☐ Uses some **supporting arguments & ideas** of good quality that build audience some interest or help a bit with understanding; establishes some pathos.	☐ Uses few or no **supporting arguments & ideas**; ideas are of poor quality, do not build audience interest/ knowledge; limited or not pathos.
	☐ Ethically uses **more than the required #** of **external sources & evidence** derived from current, relevant high-quality research. ☐ Verbally cites and qualifies all sources.	☐ Ethically uses **at least the required #** of **external evidence & sources** derived from good quality research. ☐ Verbally cites all sources.	☐ Uses **less than the required #** of **sources**; poor source ethos. ☐ Does not verbally cite all sources.

47

Student Name(s): _____ Section:_____

	Excellent	Average	Needs Improvement
Thorough Development of Content *(cont....)*	❑ Appropriate **word choice** that is vivid and effectively expresses the speaker ideas. ❑ Language is linked to both the speaker and audience and builds credibility.	❑ **Word choice** is appropriate for the speaker and the audience; but language could be more vivid or effectively express ideas.	❑ **Word choice** is not appropriate and/or language use is not vivid or effective.
	❑ **Audio/visual aids** greatly improve listener comprehension and retention of the message. ❑ **Audio/visual aids** adhere to all communication design criteria. **(PPT aids evaluated on separate form)**	❑ **Audio/visual aids** improve listener memory or comprehension, but could be improved or violate some design criteria. **(PPT aids evaluated on separate form)**	❑ **Audio/visual aids** distract or violate significant design criteria. **(PPT evaluated on separate form)**
	❑ Stays within required **time** limits.		❑ Does not stay within required **time** limits.
Delivery			
Effective Style	❑ Makes effective and appropriate **appearance** choices including clothing (business-casual) and grooming.	❑ **Appearance**, clothing, or grooming are not quite appropriate.	❑ Clearly inappropriate **appearance** choices for the assignment.
	❑ **Facial expressions** link to the message and reflect engagement with the audience.	❑ **Facial expressions** are appropriate but could better connect to the message or audience.	❑ **Facial expressions** are ineffective or inappropriate.
	❑ Maintains direct **eye contact** in a way that engages and interacts with the audience ❑ Holds contact through audience feedback.	❑ Makes some **eye contact**, but is not fully engaged or only directs eye contact to part of the audience.	❑ Makes little to no **eye contact**.
	❑ Uses **limited notes/outline** in an effective way that enhances verbal and nonverbal engagement.	❑ Uses **limited outline/notes** but remains tied to notes in a way that interferes with other delivery elements.	❑ **Outline/notes** inhibit other delivery elements.
	❑ Physical **gestures** emphasize important points and/or transitions, engage listeners, reflect a speaker who is comfortable and at ease. ❑ Select **movement** helps to engage the audience.	❑ Speaker makes an effort with **gestures** and/or physical **movement**, but they do not serve to engage listeners or reinforce the message.	❑ **Gestures** and/or **movements** are overly distracting or ineffective.
	❑ **Volume** is appropriate to the message, audience, room, and mood.	❑ **Volume** is too strong or too soft, or is not appropriate to rhetorical situation.	❑ Speaker **volume** overwhelms the audience or the message cannot be heard.
	❑ **Speaking rate/pace** enhances the message and engages the audience.	❑ **Speaking pace** is overall or in parts either a bit too fast or slow.	❑ **Pace** is either so speedy or slow that it significantly inhibits the message.
	❑ Overall **articulation** and **enunciation** strengthen the clarity of the message. ❑ All terms and names are correctly **pronounced**.	❑ Issues with **articulation** makes it hard to distinguish words and/ or limited **enunciation** inhibits message clarity in parts of the speech. ❑ Some terms incorrectly **pronounced**.	❑ Overall poor **articulation** and/or **enunciation** throughout the speech. ❑ Significant **pronunciation** issues.
	❑ **Vocal tone** adds warmth and interest, helps entice the audience.	❑ Speaker has some **tonal variety**, but could use improvement.	❑ **Monotone** delivery style or **distracting vocal elements**.
	❑ Speaker maintains a **conversational delivery** throughout the speech.	❑ Speaker achieves **conversational delivery** at times, but needs consistency.	❑ Delivery is not **conversational**.
	❑ Speaker is **enthusiastic**. ❑ Speaker is **confident**.	❑ Displays some **enthusiasm**. ❑ Exhibits some **confidence**.	❑ Speaker is **not enthusiastic**. ❑ Speaker is **not confident**.
Group *(optional)*	❑ Group delivery is consistent, well-rehearsed, and flows as a single speech.	❑ Group delivery is somewhat inconsistent, lacks rehearsal, and/or does not flow as a speech.	❑ Group delivery is inconsistent, unrehearsed, and/or does not flow as a single speech.
Comments *(optional)*			

2014-2015 SPK 230 Speech Evaluation Form

Name(s): _____ Section: ___ Speech length: _____ Grade: ___ / ___

Speech Purpose/Type: _____ Preparation materials (optional): _____ / _____

	Excellent	Average	Needs Improvement
Organization			
Basic Intro. Elements	☐ **Opening/ attention-getter** effectively draws in the the audience to the topic in a compelling, unique, and inviting manner.	☐ **Opening/ attention-getter** is clearly identifiable, but does not draw in the audience in a compelling, unique, or inviting manner; distracts the audience or needs some development.	☐ **Opening/ attention-getter** is not present, is unrelated to the thesis argument, or significantly distracts the audience.
	☐ Speaker effectively establishes his or her **credibility** to speak on the topic.	☐ Speaker cites credentials or research, but not effectively establish **credibility** to present the topic.	☐ There is no **credibility** statement.
	☐ The speaker effectively establishes why the message is relevant to the audience/ **WIIFM**.	☐ The speaker does not clearly establish the **WIIFM** message to the audience.	☐ There is no **WIIFM** statement or it detracts from the message.
	☐ The **thesis** statement articulates an argument that clearly reflects the rhetorical purpose of the speech.	☐ The **thesis** statement is ambiguous or unfocused, or does not clearly reflect the purpose of the speech.	☐ There is no clear **thesis** statement.
	☐ **Preview** is a very brief statement that identifies the subject of each main point, in the order in which they will be presented in the speech.	☐ **Preview** is hard for the audience to identify, is not presented in the same order as the main points, or is lengthy.	☐ There is no **preview** or the preview is presented in a broad, generalized statement.
Well Organized Speech Body	☐ **Main points** effectively use an easily-identifiable organizational pattern (chronological, motivated sequence, etc.) appropriate for the rhetorical purpose; Internal details are clearly organized.	☐ **Main points** are clearly identifiable, but are not arranged according to a specific pattern; Internal information is not organized in an obvious structure.	☐ **Main points** are not identifiable, blend together, and/or are not arranged according to a specific pattern; Internal details show no organizational order.
	☐ (optional) Clearly and effectively asks the audience to **take a specific action**.	☐ (optional) **Action** request is ambiguous, or not audience specific.	☐ (optional) The **action** request is missing or not feasible.
	☐ **Transitions** make clear, brief links between main points using claim keywords; **internal transitions** are used within main points to organize and link sub-points.	☐ **Transitions** are identifiable but lengthy, ambiguous, or use terminology not linked to claims; **internal transitions** are difficult to identify.	☐ **Transitions** are not present or difficult to identify; **internal transitions** are missing.
Basic Conc. Elements	☐ Briefly **summarizes** main points in order and using claim language.	☐ **Summarizes** each main point, but the review is hard to identify, not linked to claim language, or is not presented in the same order as the main points.	☐ There is no **summary**, or summary is presented in a broad, generalized statement.
	☐ **Closing** effectively wraps up the speech by linking to the opening and leaving a lasting impression.	☐ **Clincher** is identifiable, but does not leave a lasting impression or link to the opening.	☐ There is no clear **clincher**, and/or the speech ends abruptly.
Content			
Thorough Development of Content	☐ Effectively focuses the topic and content of the speech toward a **specific audience**.	☐ Either the topic or the content does not take the **audience** into consideration.	☐ The **audience** is not taken into consideration.
	☐ **Arguments/ claims are well developed.** Main points are framed by strong claims/ arguments that support the thesis, sub-points effectively support the arguments contained in the main points.	☐ **Arguments/claims are ambiguous**, unfocused, or do not support the thesis; sub-points support of the claims needs clarity.	☐ **Arguments/ claims are missing or ineffective**; sub-points or do not support claims.
	☐ Uses significant **supporting arguments & ideas** (e.g., analogies, narratives, statistics, testimony, etc.) of the highest quality that build audience interest and enhance understanding; establishes strong pathos.	☐ Uses some **supporting arguments & ideas** of good quality that build audience some interest or help a bit with understanding; establishes some pathos.	☐ Uses few or no **supporting arguments & ideas**; ideas are of poor quality, do not build audience interest/ knowledge; limited or not pathos.
	☐ Ethically uses **more than the required #** of **external sources & evidence** derived from current, relevant high-quality research. ☐ Verbally cites and qualifies all sources.	☐ Ethically uses **at least the required #** of **external evidence & sources** derived from good quality research. ☐ Verbally cites all sources.	☐ Uses **less than the required #** of **sources**; poor source ethos. ☐ Does not verbally cite all sources.

Student Name(s): _____   Section:_____

	Excellent	Average	Needs Improvement
Thorough Development of Content *(cont....)*	❏ Appropriate **word choice** that is vivid and effectively expresses the speaker ideas. ❏ Language is linked to both the speaker and audience and builds credibility.	❏ **Word choice** is appropriate for the speaker and the audience; but language could be more vivid or effectively express ideas.	❏ **Word choice** is not appropriate and/or language use is not vivid or effective.
	❏ **Audio/visual aids** greatly improve listener comprehension and retention of the message. ❏ **Audio/visual aids** adhere to all communication design criteria. **(PPT aids evaluated on separate form)**	❏ **Audio/visual aids** improve listener memory or comprehension, but could be improved or violate some design criteria. **(PPT aids evaluated on separate form)**	❏ **Audio/visual aids** distract or violate significant design criteria. **(PPT evaluated on separate form)**
	❏ Stays within required **time** limits.		❏ Does not stay within required **time** limits.

		Delivery	

	Excellent	Average	Needs Improvement
Effective Style	❏ Makes effective and appropriate **appearance** choices including clothing (business-casual) and grooming.	❏ **Appearance**, clothing, or grooming are not quite appropriate.	❏ Clearly inappropriate **appearance** choices for the assignment.
	❏ **Facial expressions** link to the message and reflect engagement with the audience.	❏ **Facial expressions** are appropriate but could better connect to the message or audience.	❏ **Facial expressions** are ineffective or inappropriate.
	❏ Maintains direct **eye contact** in a way that engages and interacts with the audience ❏ Holds contact through audience feedback.	❏ Makes some **eye contact**, but is not fully engaged or only directs eye contact to part of the audience.	❏ Makes little to no **eye contact**.
	❏ Uses **limited notes/outline** in an effective way that enhances verbal and nonverbal engagement.	❏ Uses **limited outline/notes** but remains tied to notes in a way that interferes with other delivery elements.	❏ **Outline/notes** inhibit other delivery elements.
	❏ Physical **gestures** emphasize important points and/or transitions, engage listeners, reflect a speaker who is comfortable and at ease. ❏ Select **movement** helps to engage the audience.	❏ Speaker makes an effort with **gestures** and/or physical **movement**, but they do not serve to engage listeners or reinforce the message.	❏ **Gestures** and/or **movements** are overly distracting or ineffective.
	❏ **Volume** is appropriate to the message, audience, room, and mood.	❏ **Volume** is too strong or too soft, or is not appropriate to rhetorical situation.	❏ Speaker **volume** overwhelms the audience or the message cannot be heard.
	❏ **Speaking rate/pace** enhances the message and engages the audience.	❏ **Speaking pace** is overall or in parts either a bit too fast or slow.	❏ **Pace** is either so speedy or slow that it significantly inhibits the message.
	❏ Overall **articulation** and **enunciation** strengthen the clarity of the message. ❏ All terms and names are correctly **pronounced**.	❏ Issues with **articulation** makes it hard to distinguish words and/ or limited **enunciation** inhibits message clarity in parts of the speech. ❏ Some terms incorrectly **pronounced**.	❏ Overall poor **articulation** and/or **enunciation** throughout the speech. ❏ Significant **pronunciation** issues.
	❏ **Vocal tone** adds warmth and interest, helps entice the audience.	❏ Speaker has some **tonal variety**, but could use improvement.	❏ **Monotone** delivery style or **distracting vocal elements**.
	❏ Speaker maintains a **conversational delivery** throughout the speech.	❏ Speaker achieves **conversational delivery** at times, but needs consistency.	❏ Delivery is not **conversational**.
	❏ Speaker is **enthusiastic**. ❏ Speaker is **confident**.	❏ Displays some **enthusiasm**. ❏ Exhibits some **confidence**.	❏ Speaker is **not enthusiastic**. ❏ Speaker is **not confident**.
Group *(optional)*	❏ Group delivery is consistent, well-rehearsed, and flows as a single speech.	❏ Group delivery is somewhat inconsistent, lacks rehearsal, and/or does not flow as a speech.	❏ Group delivery is inconsistent, unrehearsed, and/or does not flow as a single speech.
Comments *(optional)*			

2014-2015 PowerPoint Slides Evaluation Form

Student Name(s): _____   Section: _____   Speech Type: _____   Grade: _____

	Excellent	Above Average – Below Average	Needs Significant Improvement
Audience Connection	___ Slides have a clear visual link to the audience in a significant and meaningful manner that does not distract from the message.	___ Slides somewhat visually link to the audience or do so in some way that distracts from the message.	___ Slides do not visually link to the audience or do so in a way that significantly distracts from the message.
Linked to Speech	___ Slides are completely connected to the verbal presentation in order, logos, and purpose.	___ At points, the slides are not connected to the verbal presentation in order, logos, and/or purpose.	___ Slides do not follow the order, purpose, or logos of the speech.
Consistency	___ Slides have a consistent look and feel with design, image types, use of text and visual elements.	___ Slides do not have a consistent look and feel with some elements of the design, image types, use of text and visual elements.	___ There is no clear consistency with the look and feel with most elements, the design, image types, use of text and/or visual elements.
Layout	___ Construction of the visual and textual elements guides the eye, has clear contrast, and fills the slide without cluttering it.	___ Construction of the visual and textual elements do not clearly guide the eye (either cluttered or empty; element placement somewhat distracts) and lacks contrast	___ Construction of the visual and textual elements do not guide the eye and are significantly cluttered or empty; there is poor overall contrast between elements.
Text	___ Text is very limited, visible in size and font (typically san serif), there are no typos or orphans.	___ Text is somewhat heavy and/or not always visible due to size or font; there are some typos or orphans.	___ Text is heavy and/or mostly not visible due to size or font; there are significant typos or orphans.
Images	___ Slides are MOSTLY visual rather than textual or empty in nature and use high quality images through the entire presentation.	___ Slides use several visual images or a moderate amount of visual images; some images lack visual quality; slide visuals are not the predominant element of the visual aid.	___ Slides use limited to no visual images; most to all images lack visual quality.
Animation & Transitions	___ (optional) Element animation and slide transitions are all useful and never distract.	___ (optional) Animations and/or slide transitions do not always seem useful and distract to some degree.	___ (optional) Element animation and/or slide are not clearly useful for the presentation and are a significant distraction.
Delivery	___ Presenters are interactive with slides rather than using them as a backdrop; presenters stay in sync with slides, do not block images, effectively incorporate any video inside slides, and use the software effectively.	___ Presenters are somewhat to not very interactive with the slides; slides at times or often appear to be only a backdrop; video is not effectively incorporated inside slides, slides are not in sync or not always shown consistently or effectively.	___ Presenters use slides only as a backdrop; slides are blocked or not in sync with the verbal presentation; videos are not shown within the slides or in a distracting manner; slides use is distracting in a significant way.
Comprehension	___ Slides significantly help the audience with comprehension of the verbal message.	___ Slides help the audience with comprehension only somewhat or not very much.	___ Slides do not help the audience with comprehension of the verbal presentation.

Comments (optional): _____

56

2014-2015 PowerPoint Slides Evaluation Form

Student Name(s): _____   Section: _____   Speech Type: _____   Grade: _____

	Excellent	Above Average – Below Average	Needs Significant Improvement
Audience Connection	___ Slides have a clear visual link to the audience in a significant and meaningful manner that does not distract from the message.	___ Slides somewhat visually link to the audience or do so in some way that distracts from the message.	___ Slides do not visually link to the audience or do so in a way that significantly distracts from the message.
Linked to Speech	___ Slides are completely connected to the verbal presentation in order, logos, and purpose.	___ At points, the slides are not connected to the verbal presentation in order, logos, and/or purpose.	___ Slides do not follow the order, purpose, or logos of the speech.
Consistency	___ Slides have a consistent look and feel with design, image types, use of text and visual elements.	___ Slides do not have a consistent look and feel with some elements of the design, image types, use of text and visual elements.	___ There is no clear consistency with the look and feel with most elements, the design, image types, use of text and/or visual elements.
Layout	___ Construction of the visual and textual elements guides the eye, has clear contrast, and fills the slide without cluttering it.	___ Construction of the visual and textual elements do not clearly guide the eye (either cluttered or empty; element placement somewhat distracts) and lacks contrast	___ Construction of the visual and textual elements do not guide the eye and are significantly cluttered or empty; there is poor overall contrast between elements.
Text	___ Text is very limited, visible in size and font (typically san serif), there are no typos or orphans.	___ Text is somewhat heavy and/or not always visible due to size or font; there are some typos or orphans.	___ Text is heavy and/or mostly not visible due to size or font; there are significant typos or orphans.
Images	___ Slides are MOSTLY visual rather than textual or empty in nature and use high quality images through the entire presentation.	___ Slides use several visual images or a moderate amount of visual images; some images lack visual quality; slide visuals are not the predominant element of the visual aid.	___ Slides use limited to no visual images; most to all images lack visual quality.
Animation & Transitions	___ (optional) Element animation and slide transitions are all useful and never distract.	___ (optional) Animations and/or slide transitions do not always seem useful and distract to some degree.	___ (optional) Element animation and/or slide are not clearly useful for the presentation and are a significant distraction.
Delivery	___ Presenters are interactive with slides rather than using them as a backdrop; presenters stay in sync with slides, do not block images, effectively incorporate any video inside slides, and use the software effectively.	___ Presenters are somewhat to not very interactive with the slides; slides at times or often appear to be only a backdrop; video is not effectively incorporated inside slides, slides are not in sync or not always shown consistently or effectively.	___ Presenters use slides only as a backdrop; slides are blocked or not in sync with the verbal presentation; videos are not shown within the slides or in a distracting manner; slides use is distracting in a significant way.
Comprehension	___ Slides significantly help the audience with comprehension of the verbal message.	___ Slides help the audience with comprehension only somewhat or not very much.	___ Slides do not help the audience with comprehension of the verbal presentation.

Comments (optional): _____

_____

2014-2015 SPK 230 Interview Evaluation Form

Student Name: _____ Section: _____ Prep Materials (optional): _____ Grade: _____

	Excellent : You get a job offer!	Average: You may get called back..	Problems: You would not get this job.
First Impression	___ On time for the interview. ___ Industry related, business professional attire; does not distract; neat & well-groomed. ___ Firm handshake. ___ Introduced self with enthusiasm, warmth, and interest. ___ Smiled; excellent eye contact. ___ Waited to be invited to sit.	___ Industry is not clearly related, business linked or could be improved. ___ Shook hands. ___ Introduced self. ___ Limited enthusiasm. ___ Sat without being invited to do so.	___ Late for the interview. ___ Attire is not at all business linked. ___ Unkempt grooming or heavy scent. ___ No handshake. ___ No introduction. ___ Did not smile or show enthusiasm. ___ No eye contact.
Interview Interaction (Verbal/Content)	___ Answers are well-organized. ___ Answers show clear knowledge of as well as a link to the company, position, and industry. ___ Answers engage through specific and vivid details in narrative or examples that demonstrate the applicant's qualities as they pertain to the job. ___ Answers reflect résumé details. ___ Used a respectful tone. ___ Does not interrupt; shows listening feedback (e.g., summarizing, asking questions). ___ Language is appropriate for a professional interaction. ___ Confident without bragging. ___ Strong verbal enthusiasm. ___ Used effective volume & pace. ___ Clarified any misunderstandings. ___ Asked questions as appropriate and relevant.	___ Answers need some organization. ___ Answers show some knowledge. ___ Answers engage through specific and vivid details but could do better to demonstrate applicant qualities. ___ Answers do little to reflect résumé. ___ Some disrespectful or culturally insensitive language. ___ Some interrupting or not listening. ___ Language is not quite appropriate. ___ Lacking confidence or some bragging. ___ Little verbal enthusiasm. ___ Used a good volume & pace.	___ Answers are not well-organized. ___ Answers do not show clear knowledge. ___ Few or no stories or examples. ___ Answers not linked to résumé. ___ Used a disrespectful tone. ___ Interrupts/ does not listen. ___ Language is inappropriate. ___ Not confident or brags. ___ No verbal enthusiasm. ___ Problems with volume or pace. ___ Need to ask appropriate questions.
Interview Interaction (Non-verbal)	___ Demonstrates strong non-verbal listening feedback (e.g., nod, smile, eye contact). ___ Eye contact with any speaker or interviewer. ___ Facial expressions link to tone & show engagement. ___ Excellent posture. ___ Lack of fidgeting or distracting behavior. ___ Gestures engage, reinforce the message, do not distract.	___ Some non-verbal listening feedback ___ Not always making strong eye contact. ___ Some linked facial expressions. ___ Some fidgeting or distracting behavior. ___ Limited engaging gestures.	___ Little/no non-verbal listening feedback ___ Little/no eye contact. ___ Facial expressions not linked. ___ Poor posture. ___ Very distracting non-verbal behavior.
Closing	___ Offered thanks. ___ Firm handshake. ___ Clarifies the interview timeline/follow-up. ___ Shows respect and strong job enthusiasm.	___ Handshake. ___ Not clear interview follow-up offered.	___ Did not offer thanks. ___ No handshake. ___ No interview timeline/follow-up. ___ Little job enthusiasm.

Comments (optional): _____